Land Rights

Timothy Chesters is Lecturer in Modern Languages at Royal Holloway, University of London.

The Oxford Amnesty Lectures is a registered charity. Its purpose is to raise funds to increase awareness of Amnesty International in the academic and wider communities. It is otherwise independent of Amnesty International. It began as a fund-raising project for the local Amnesty group in Oxford, and is now one of the world's leading name-lecture series. To date, Oxford Amnesty Lectures has raised around £100,000 for Amnesty International.

Land Rights

The Oxford Amnesty Lectures 2005

Edited by

Timothy Chesters

OXFORD
UNIVERSITY PRESS

OXFORD
UNIVERSITY PRESS

Great Clarendon Street, Oxford OX2 6DP

Oxford University Press is a department of the University of Oxford.
It furthers the University's objective of excellence in research, scholarship,
and education by publishing worldwide in

Oxford New York

Auckland Cape Town Dar es Salaam Hong Kong Karachi
Kuala Lumpur Madrid Melbourne Mexico City Nairobi
New Delhi Shanghai Taipei Toronto

With offices in

Argentina Austria Brazil Chile Czech Republic France Greece
Guatemala Hungary Italy Japan Poland Portugal Singapore
South Korea Switzerland Thailand Turkey Ukraine Vietnam

Published in the United States
by Oxford University Press Inc., New York

First published 2009

British Library Cataloguing in Publication Data
Data available

Library of Congress Cataloging in Publication Data
Data available

Typeset by SPI Publisher Services, Pondicherry, India
Printed in Great Britain
on acid-free paper by
Clays Ltd., St Ives plc.

ISBN 978-0-19-954510-0

1 3 5 7 9 10 8 6 4 2

Preface

The 13th Oxford Amnesty Lectures, on the subject of 'Land Rights', were given in January, February, and March 2005. Seven speakers addressed the series: Marilyn Strathern, Misha Glenny, Romeo Saganash, Frank Brennan, Ken Wiwa, Richard Leakey, and Daniel Baron-Cohen. I would like on behalf of Oxford Amnesty Lectures to express my thanks to all of them. Not all the lectures are reproduced in this book. Misha Glenny's contribution is under copyright; Daniel Baron-Cohen's was heavily image-based and so, while extremely well-received as an occasion, deemed unsuitable for publication here. That leaves five lectures, with an additional guest contribution from William Beinart. To him too go my thanks. In the spirit of dialogue and debate traditionally championed by Oxford Amnesty Lectures, this book also includes five responses to each of our speakers. The respondents were: Laura Rival, Ellen L. Lutz, Marcus Colchester, Adam Higazi, and Lotte Hughes. I am grateful to all of them for their thought-provoking and, on occasion, provocative companion pieces. Final thanks go to the other members of the Oxford Amnesty Lectures committee, whose hard work made the lectures, and so this book, possible. They are Melissa McCarthy, Chris Miller, Nicholas Owen, Fabienne Pagnier, Deana Rankin, Richard Scholar, Stephen Shute, Kate Tunstall, Katrin Wehling, and Wes Williams.

T.G.C.

Contents

Contributors

WILLIAM BEINART is Rhodes Professor of Race Relations at St Anthony's College, Oxford. His most recent books include the second edition of his *Twentieth-Century South Africa* (2001) and *The Rise of Conservation in South Africa*, 1770–1950 (2003).

FRANK BRENNAN is a Jesuit priest and Professor of Law in the Institute of Legal Studies at the Australian Catholic University. He is an officer of the Order of Australia for services to Aboriginal Australians.

TIMOTHY CHESTERS is a lecturer in Modern Languages at Royal Holloway, University of London. He is a specialist in the relationship between learned demonology and culture in early modern Europe.

MARCUS COLCHESTER is director of the Forest Peoples' Programme. He joint-edited *The Struggle for Land and the Fate of the Forests* (1993).

ADAM HIGAZI is a doctoral student in African studies at the Department for International Development, University of Oxford. He is currently preparing a thesis on 'The Historical Ethnography of Conflict in Plateau State, Central Nigeria'.

LOTTE HUGHES is a lecturer in African Arts and Cultures at the Open University's Ferguson Centre for African and Asian Studies. She is author of *The No-nonsense Guide to Indigenous People* (2003) and *Moving the Maasai: A Colonial Misadventure* (2006).

RICHARD LEAKEY is a paleoanthropologist and former director of the Kenya Wildlife Service. In 1999 he was appointed Cabinet Secretary and head of the civil service, a post he resigned in 2001. His books include *The Origin of Humankind* (1994) and (with Roger Lewin) *The Sixth Extinction: Patterns of Life and the Future of Mankind* (1995).

Ellen L. Lutz is Executive Director of Cultural Survival. She has written widely on human rights and conflict resolution, with particular reference to Latin America. She is author of *Serving Survivors of Torture* (1991).

Laura Rival is a fellow of Linacre College, Oxford, and a university lecturer in Anthropology and Development. Her work centres on the impact of development policies on Amerindian indigenous peoples. She is author of *Trekking through History: The Huaorani of Amazonian Ecuador* (2002).

Romeo Saganash is a lawyer, director of Québec relations for the Cree Regional Authority and former Deputy Grand Chief of the Grand Council of the Crees.

Marilyn Strathern is William Wyse Professor of Social Anthropology at the University of Cambridge, and Mistress of Girton College. She is author of *Property, Substance and Effect: Anthropological Essays on Persons and Things* (1999) and *Kinship, Law and the Unexpected: Relatives are Often a Surprise* (2005).

Ken Wiwa, also known as Ken Saro-Wiwa Jnr., is a Canada-based Nigerian journalist and writer. He is author of *In the Shadow of the Saint* (2000). He currently writes as a columnist for the Toronto *Globe and Mail.*

Introduction

Timothy Chesters

Indigenous peoples and governments, industrialists and environmentalists all use—or have at some stage to confront—the language of 'land rights'. But what does it mean to invoke that language? What kind of problems can it help us to solve? The papers collected in this volume, a selection of the lectures given at the Oxford Amnesty Lectures series on 'land rights' held in Oxford in Spring 2005, offer a range of reflections on land, rights, and how we might connect the two.

This connection is not obvious. Rights *of* the land or rights *to* the land? Genitive or dative? The choice of preposition muddies the stream, and neither has achieved the complete exclusion of the other. Conservationists and ecologists sometimes call—whether explicitly or implicitly—on the rights *of* the land: not to be exploited, for example, or polluted or despoiled. Propping up this genitive use is a straightforward derivation from the more usual 'human rights': just as 'human rights' describes the rights of the human, so 'land rights', one might think, should describe the rights of the land. Logical as this may seem, this kind of transferral requires a bold leap of faith, perhaps a leap even bolder than that which allows us to speak, similarly, of 'animal rights'. For while an animistic view of land, such as prevails in certain traditional societies and some parts of the environmentalist movement, might happily invest land with a desire to demand its rights (as well as its rites), those who defer to the secular, humanist origins of rights-speak have usually fought shy of extending that language beyond the purely human sphere. It is notable that only Richard Leakey, in the papers that follow, comes close to invoking 'land rights' as the rights *of* the land.

The more widely accepted sense of 'land rights' refers, rather, to rights *to* the land. This 'to' marks a claim, straightforwardly, on the thing itself. But it also seems to await completion by a verb: rights to inhabit the land, to farm it, build homes upon it, also to mine it, fell its trees, or extract its oil. Here too a danger lurks. Whereas those who deify the land invest it with an agency at odds with the rationalist rights tradition, those who speak in this way risk robbing it of any agency at all. Land becomes something done to and not doing—a passive commodity with no right of reply. Of course, the effects of climate change and environmental catastrophe may yet, through nature's vengeance, provide a painful corrective to this view. In the meantime, however, the language of 'rights to' can make life easy for the colonizer's dollar. As soon as we make of land a stake passively awaiting claimants, we are already on the way to accepting the equation of land and property, with all the Western legal strictures that property, and 'property rights', imply. This development was probably inevitable, and most indigenous movements have now accepted that their battles must be fought on these terms or not at all. But since this acceptance already marks a considerable concession, it should warn us against too vaunting a claim for the language of 'land rights'.

Compounding the problem for those of us in the West is that much current leftist discourse (and not only 'rights' discourse) has a determinedly secondary way of talking about land. Postmodern theory as practised in my own discipline, literary and cultural criticism, is a case in point. A quick look at the Arts faculty notice-board (or the contents pages of many academic journals) will confirm that those of us with an interest in identity politics of various kinds have become extremely fluent in the language of *space*: 'limits', 'margins', 'borders', 'deviation', 'liminality', 'transgression' or (to take the title of the previous Oxford Amnesty Lectures series), 'displacement'. Indeed, it seems that in this post-Foucauldian era, it has become difficult to imagine the relation between the powerful and powerless in anything other than spatial terms. From this one might suppose that postmodern theory would have much to say on that particular form of space to which we point when we say 'land'. But postmodern 'space' and 'land' are not the same. Indeed, our talk of the first may have prevailed at the expense of the second.

The postmodern language of 'space'—understood as the dimension, or theatre, in which subjects fight for power—is metaphorical and superstructural. Metaphorical, because even though postmodern 'space' frequently instantiates itself in a material environment (as in the notorious panopticon described by Foucault in *Discipline and Punish*), it often floats free of, even flouts, the physical landscape. For instance, it is primarily a metaphor that postmodernist historians intend when they speak of homosexuals, criminals, and the mentally ill as 'marginalized' subjects. For whereas these characters may at various times throughout history have been consigned to the physical edges of their societies—as when all three were locked up in Bicêtre on the outskirts of eighteenth-century Paris—many lived and worked, after all, at the literal centres of politico-cultural power. In related fashion, postmodern 'space' has become, chiefly at least, a superstructural dimension. Even in postcolonial theory (the one area that might have been expected to develop an account of land and landlessness) there exists a tendency to count the superstructural costs of land dispossession while showing rather less interest in the material losses at the base. Enquiries into representations of land, labour, and resources were once of great interest to Marxist literary theorists, such as the Raymond Williams of *The Country and the City*. Today these have largely been buried beneath questions of colonized ethnic, gender, or linguistic identities. To say as much is neither to devalue the considerable achievements of postcolonial theory nor to belittle the importance of identity politics. It is rather to note how far the current hegemony of 'space'-speak has tended to exclude issues of land from (to use another favourite spatial metaphor) the 'discursive territory' of postmodern theory.

Land is neither a superstructural nor a metaphorical concept. For the contributors to this volume, the primary stake in struggles for land rights is economic before it is cultural. And, as is clear from the first contribution, by Marilyn Strathern, those whose land is under threat tend rather to view it in metonymic terms. Her essay invites us to follow the Troubriand islanders in 'looking at one thing and seeing another'. Being looked at are natural resources, trees or yams; being seen is the creative force of the land that produced them. Thanks to this metonymic 'double vision', which Strathern claims to be fundamental to Melanesian ways of seeing the world, the tangible fruits of the land become expressive both of land's own creative potential and of the complex and intangible social relationships, and sense of personal and communal worth, upon which their harvest depends. In this way the products of the land are experienced as extensions of the land, and of its human stewardship, just as a book may be seen as an extension of its writer's creativity. This comparison is not an idle one for Strathern, for she uses it as a basis on which to argue that the relationship between land and its creations in Papua New Guinea might be construed, in Western terms, as analagous to that between authors and intellectual property. This is a tempting possibility, since it offers up a means by which indigenous populations might lay claim to land as a special form of property, and not merely one transactable in the developers' terms of brute commodity value. It is not without its problems, however. As Laura Rival writes in her response to Strathern's paper, a fully historicized account of land claims would have to take account of the fact that, even within indigenous communities, the creative potential of land 'is subject to multiple and overlapping claims of ownership' by social actors who are 'not economically or politically equal'. That this situation has arisen at all is testament to the power of a corporate view of land which has succeeded in fragmenting notions of common land through the 'rise of exclusive, calculative, modes of valuation'.

Romeo Saganash's lecture also takes up the theme of individual versus collective claims on land, here in the framework of international human rights. A lawyer and spokesman for the James Bay Cree people, Saganash contends that attempts to incorporate the notion of collective rights in the long-debated UN draft Declaration on the Rights of indigenous Peoples have foundered on what he considers to be the discriminatory objections of (among others) the UK's Foreign and Commonwealth Office. While successive UK officials have acknowledged the importance of collective rights, they have at the same time sought to segregate those rights from the international human rights framework, claiming that human rights can only properly be asserted by individuals, not groups. Saganash takes careful issue with this position, arguing that such an understanding contravenes the spirit of the UN Charter, as well as the principles of numerous other working groups on Land Rights, treaty monitoring bodies, and international convenants (such as the International Covenant on Civil and Political Rights and the International Convention on the Elimination of All Forms of Racial Discrimination). In her response to Saganash's paper, Ellen Lutz reports that, in spring 2006, the newly formed United Nations Human Rights Council finalized its draft Declaration on the Rights of indigenous Peoples and forwarded it to the United Nations General Assembly for approval in December of the same year. In itself a great step forward, the Declaration met further difficulties when, at the December meeting the General Assembly declined to approve it. Reasons for this setback were various. Some African states regretted that it failed to provide a satisfactory definition of 'indigenous'. They were also nervous that it seemed to promise 'self-determination' for some indigenous peoples, arguing that, while useful in colonial / postcolonial contexts, such promises made little global sense in a continent where the vast majority of Africans might be deemed 'indigenous'. Overall, however, the most vociferous opposition came from those states, identified in Saganash's lecture, which had opposed the draft declaration all along. We await further developments.

Frank Brennan, a Jesuit priest and lawyer, addresses the same tension between individual and collective rights in the context of Australian Aboriginal land rights. Whereas Saganash focusses on the international human rights context, Brennan gives us a national perspective. In a detailed study of Australian developments over the last forty years, Brennan argues that there has indeed been a delicate balance to be struck between Aboriginal claims to land title and self-determination on the one hand, and on the other the rights of indigenous individuals to enjoy the same legal protections—for instance, equal pay, or access to education and healthcare—as the white population. The need for such a balance is inevitable in a country whose indigenous population lives in two polities simultaneously and, as Brennan shows, neither legislators nor campaigners have always got it right. The 'realists', who argue that the Aboriginal life will only improve once it is granted the protections offered by the nation state, must face up to the many failures of this approach in practice, from the economic consequences of equal pay for pastoralists in the Northern Territory, to the disastrous results of well-intentioned, but ill-conceived, welfare provision. Meanwhile, the 'idealists' have argued the only way for Aborigines to stake their land claims is to insist on a form of cultural separatism. Their ambition, Brennan argues, must contend with a range of Aboriginal practices—spearing as punishment, the position of Aboriginal women—that contravene even the most basic of individual rights. While the ongoing negotiation between these two positions is crowded with difficulties, he claims, it can only be right that the voices of indigenous actors are heard. Self-determination for the indigenous population, which is to say the freedom to fashion a life in the two polities while shutting the door on neither, is a fraught but necessary step towards an Australia in which all people—white and indigenous alike—might come to terms with their own history. In his response to Brennan's piece, Marcus Colchester largely agrees. However, Colchester cautions against too conflictual a view of the relation between the individual and the collective, claiming that communities' claim to land rights need not threaten the rights of the individual. Echoing Saganash and Lutz, he argues that it has been precisely by over-emphasizing the supposed non-commensurability of the two regimes that opponents of the draft Declaration on the Rights of indigenous

Peoples, including the UK government, have been able to block progress on the international scene.

Ken Wiwa switches the arena of struggle to Africa, the scene of our final three contributions. Wiwa's own paper concentrates on the plight of the Ogoni people of the Niger Delta, whose land and resources have been the stake in a long campaign over which Wiwa's own father, Ken Saro-Wiwa, presided before his execution by the Nigerian authorities in the summer of 1995. Here too the plea is for recognition of collective rights to land, in this case land despoiled by decades of exploitation at the hands of multinational oil companies, most notably Shell, working with the blessing of the Nigerian government. Saganash and Brennan focused on the tension—whether real or imagined—between communal rights and the rights of the individual. In contrast, Wiwa's anxieties spring from his own people's inability to express exactly what is at stake in such collective rights. For him what is stake is the story through which the Ogoni might come to narrate their own losses. What the Ogoni currently lack, and sorely need, is what Wiwa calls a 'cultural inventory' of what they have, and what might still be taken from them. Only then, he argues, might they make their case against the despoilers. However, the business of telling stories is no simple matter, especially when—as his novelist father found—telling means writing in a proud oral culture. Wiwa urges his own people that, however hallowed their oral narrative traditions, the first step to reclaiming is an act of writing down. Following in the footsteps (or as he says more ambivalently, shadow) of his father, Wiwa is the *wiayor*—the anointed, though often reluctant, storyteller—who tells his people that which they may not wish to hear. In his response to Wiwa's paper, Adam Higazi broadens the perpsective to encompass national reaction in Nigeria to the pursuits of Shell and their associates. In a finding that echoes some of the African objections to the draft Declaration on the Rights of indigenous Peoples raised at the UN General Assembly in 2006, Higazi shows that not all Nigerians are sympathetic to Ogoni claims when framed under the notion of 'indigeneity'. In the north of the country, for instance, oil is seen as part of Nigeria's national prosperity; the notion that the Ogoni might lay special claim to the proceeds, because 'indigenous' to the land from which it is taken, drops away before a competing, more nationally-oriented conception of identity.

Richard Leakey's contribution is by his own admission provocative. Combining both the palaeontologist's long view with the pragmatism of one who served for many years in the Kenyan government, Leakey argues that the very concept of 'indigenous' is problematic in a country where so many might stake a claim on that title. As Lutz argued in her response to Saganash, this argument has proved a stumbling block in many regions on the continent. And while Leakey acknowledges that many injustices in Kenya were perpetrated under British colonial rule, he argues that redressing them now through the redistribution of land title would jeopardize national unity and—by extension—attempts to represent the country's interests abroad. A further, more deep-seated, objection to indigenous land claims has its roots in Leakey's commitment to ecological conservation. Observing that 'the rights to land should not include the rights to debase it', he argues that the very concept of land ownership in Kenya has sometimes proved inimical to proper respect for the land itself, with over-grazing and resulting loss of vegetable cover leading to soil erosion in many parts of Kenya. The land too has its rights, he argues, and we do it a disservice by calling it 'ours'. In her vigorous response to Leakey's paper, Lotte Hughes finds some room for agreement, and much more for dissent. Hughes agrees that 'indigeneity' is a problematic label, and one often used by politicians to divide sections of the Kenyan population. She claims nonetheless that it is a concept worth keeping, and provides the 'widely accepted' definition provided by the UN and International Labour Organization. Also worth keeping, she argues, is the notion of 'land title', one which cannot be dismissed as easily as Leakey would like to claim. Offering as she does a historicized account of land rights in Kenya, Hughes argues that even early twentieth-century colonial administrators recognized the 'gross injustice' done to the Maasai by conceding their land to the settlers.

William Beinart's essay stays in Africa, but shifts the focus onto land reform in post-apartheid South Africa. He takes as a case study the land reform procedures put in place in the Eastern Cape province in the 1990s, a process of which he had personal experience as an adviser at the Land and Agriculture Policy Centre in Johannesburg. Beinart argues from the premise that while access to secure residential land and shelter is a basic human right, access to agricultural land is not. Nor are such government-controlled projects to grant such access to groups, rather than individuals, always viable in practice. Beinart gives the example of the communally owned trust farms which invaded state-purchased but previously unallocated land (Released Areas or RAs) in the early 1990s. It would be easy to applaud such occupations as successful results in a popular struggle for land. But Beinart argues that, in spite of its apparent attractions, the populist emphasis on 'community'—also ubiquitous among land rights NGOs—risks obscuring a number of concrete problems on the ground. In the examples cited, these included the growth in the numbers of free-range livestock and inadequate fencing (both of which threatened arable production), disagreements about settlement planning, and the trusts' inability to control the numbers of people moving to the settlement. In the light of such difficulties Beinart makes the case for a more gradualized and individualized approach to land redistribution in South Africa.

In the tradition of the Oxford Amnesty Lectures, the contributions to this volume occupy different vantage points overlooking common ground. The difference lies first of all in the variety of disciplinary or discursive perspectives offered: anthropological (Strathern, Rival, Leakey), historical (Beinart, Hughes, Higazi), legal (Saganash, Brennan), governmental (Leakey, Beinart), or activist (Saganash, Lutz, Colchester, Wiwa). The volume has also assembled contributions diverse in their geographical focus: on Asia, Canada, Australia, and Africa (East, West and South). In spite of this variety, however, several common themes—or tensions—have emerged with some insistence. These have include, but are not limited to, the tension around the concept of 'indigeneity' (Leakey, Hughes); the tension between the transactable and the non-transactable (Strathern, Rival, Wiwa); the tension between national and local conceptions of land and resource ownership (Leakey, Higazi); and the tension between communal and individual rights (Brennan, Saganash, Colchester, Lutz, Beinart). It is unlikely that any volume of essays, least of all one with such a varied focus, can realistically aspire to resolve such tensions. The best that can be hoped, perhaps, is that this book may help us feel them more keenly, in all their troubling variety, and see more clearly what is at stake in the struggles of tomorrow.

1

Land: Intangible or Tangible Property?

Marilyn Strathern

To think about land rights at once enlarges and diminishes whatever we might wish to say about human rights. It enlarges, for at its greatest extent the idea of land evokes the planet, the commonality of our existence, what we share whether we like it or not. It diminishes, insofar as land seems a particular materiality, a specific kind of resource, just one among many aspects of people's lives, and for many town-dwellers no more than a house plot or office site. I want to see if we can deal with both these dimensions at the same time.

Something of that first dimension is found in the notion that the language of land ownership is too restrictive. Or, rather, that one should think a little imaginatively about ownership. An Australian judge tried to convey how very 'other' Aboriginal concepts were from those found in the law of property, in just this vein. He concluded a famous land claims case[1] with the remark that rather than thinking of land belonging to people one should think of people belonging to the land. The people here were members of a particular clan, and this was the most succinct way in which he could summarize the totalizing effect that land had on their lives.

I had encountered almost exactly the same formulation in the work of a French anthropologist reporting on the 'Are' are people of Malaita, Solomon Islands.[2] The paramount chief dictated to him a long text explaining the different rules of Melanesian land tenure, including the nature of personal links to the land: this because that is what people's accomplishments have sprung from and where, like their ancestors, they will be buried. In this sense people own the land. But the text is preceded by an extensive explanation of how, in another sense, people do not own land at all; rather the land owns them. 'The land owns 'Are' are people', he declared. 'The land owns men and women; they are there to take care of the land.'[3] This is an appeal of an almost planetary order.

Given the dependence of these Solomon Islanders' livelihood on the gardening of root crops perhaps we should not be so surprised that they have an enlarged sense of what they owe the land. However, let me tell you where I last came across a similar phrase, this time in reference to a particular place.[4] The place is an old square in the former East Berlin, Alexanderplatz, whose reconstruction has been the subject of more than a decade of German politics. Residents mobilize a double sense of belonging: not just how Alexanderplatz belongs to them but how people belong to Alexanderplatz. This was the view of those citizens who thought their claims were being overlooked by planners, claims that were based on an embracing relationship with this place as an embodiment of a particular 'feeling of life'.[5] What gave them an entitlement to determine its future was the totality of their experiences, responsibility, knowledge, and sense of citizenship from which sprang the rights and obligations they felt towards Alexanderplatz: they were there, we could almost say, to take care of it.

This enlarged sense of what was at stake was set against what they saw as the narrow interests of investers who had acquired the land as real estate, land that could be built on and from which amenities would arise. The investors were dealing with ideas of property within a legal discourse that gave them control to determine future development. The citizen protesters were claiming something much more diffuse.[6]

But let us look at that second and apparently diminished sense of land as a resource. The planners had their own aspirations, including improvement to what seemed derelict, and the wealth creation that would come with reconstruction. They echo aspirations elsewhere that see land as an exploitable resource, appropriated for plantations or mines, bringing in revenue. And if we turn to the world that seems in need of development, whether it belongs to minorities within a nation state or to newly independent states, we know that in many places residents are keen for improvement, may seek profit for themselves. They may embrace development, as in Papua New Guinea forms of public entitlement enable clan groups to control land as a legal asset.[7]

Indeed the current concept of 'landowner' in Papua New Guinea simultaneously evokes tradition ('custom'), appealing to the depths of people's ancestral association with specific territories, while also drawing on an international language that gives them negotiating purchase with overseas companies. The Ok Tedi copper and gold mine is a case in point. Its pollution of the Fly River, one of the world's major river systems, is notorious. Equally notorious within Papua New Guinea has been the long history of local efforts to seek some kind of recompense for environmental damage and loss of livelihood.[8] But demanding recompense merges with people's own aspirations for wealth. In the expectation of the mine closing down some ten years hence, the mine continuation agreements inaugurated in 2001 incorporate all kinds of local development packages in return for consent to allow operations to continue for the moment.

So it is not just a question of enlarged and diminished apprehensions of land: there are different aspirations for it. Most stark would seem precisely to be the contrast between rights that come from *land owning the people* and those that come from *people owning the land*. On the one hand land is perceived as an embracing source not just of livelihood but of life, and not just the life of individuals but the life of society, or at its greatest extent humanity. On the other hand land is a resource that its owners can exploit, that becomes a source of wealth as well as sustenance, that can be made productive. How do we reconcile these two apparently competing views?

These are issues played out on a world scale, highly relevant to the aspirations of the international community and informing relations between the developed and developing; while Alexanderplatz reminds us that they are not tied to that, they also often inform the struggle of self-described first nations or indigenous peoples. Indeed, in the lectures to come we shall be hearing about many aspects of the way people try to talk about their humanity, their rootedness, through rights in relation to land.

I want to take advantage of some of the rich materials that it is the anthropologist's privilege to know about, where we can see global issues in microcosm. Because there are peoples, like the 'Are' are for example, who deal with something rather similar to this very contrast (land as life, land as resource) in dealing with land in their daily lives. By the same token, the radically different set of premises on which their ideas are based will give us some insight into what makes this contrast a dilemma for the international community concerned with economic and social development.

Land as Intellectual Property

I focus on a part of the world where the issues over land are less to do with the consequences of large-scale appropriations than with the exploitation of land-based resources through mining, logging, and so forth. Anticipated by the example from Ok Tedi, this is Papua New Guinea. Its two regions colonized by the Germans and British, then administered by Australia, it became independent in 1975; its five million people subsist off largely unalienated land.[9] But they do more than subsist off it. People there[10] are very interested in land as *a resource that produces resources*. This is what mobilizes their sense of entitlement and the claims they pursue in litigation, and it dominates their thinking about land rights. We should look then to the kind of produce that land yields, to its wealth-creating potential, to the way it enters into people's transactions with one another, in short, to its productivity.

Yet what we shall find is that instead of an interest in the products of the land being set *against* a cosmological concern with land as a source of life, with ancestral regeneration and custodial responsibilities,[11] the two go together. How can this be? In the same way as the Australian judge had to make play with the notion of ownership, we need to alter our understanding of 'productivity'. Suppose we talk instead of creativity. *And think of the land as creative and its products as creations.*[12]

Now I do not intend anything mystical here. If the vocabulary of creativity and creations suggests Creator deities and supreme beings that is incidental. The case I want to put is a rationalist and humanist one. I propose to draw not on the language of religion but on the language of law. Western, or as I prefer to say Euro-American, legal thinking does not just give us the notion of property in the real estate sense. There is in fact a whole class of law devoted to the issue of creativity and people's creations, although it is controversial to put it this way:[13] intellectual property rights. In the hand of lawyers[14] the application is rather technical and dry, the definition of creativity one that can be applied almost automatically, as in the supposition that the author of a work is the person who creates it. However, that is exactly the connotation I seek. The kinds of entitlements I am talking about arise in a very straightforward way from people's demonstration of their connections to land. Indeed they may think they need do no more than demonstrate a connection and entitlement is evident.[15]

I said my case was a rationalist and humanist one. That is, I do not require you to suspend disbelief in supernatural beings and mystical forces, because these hardly appear in my account. But I do require from you an imaginative leap. Two leaps in fact.

The first is that you enter into the spirit of anthropological comparison, that is, keep a sense of context and feel you can cross contexts at the same time. This is the sense in which I mobilize a contrast between two types of Euro-American property law in order to find a vocabulary with which to make credible[16] a Melanesian contrast between rights to land regarded as a source of creativity and rights to its creations. Thus the Euro-American contrast gives us the distinction between *intangible* and *tangible* property. I do not submerge the difference between these two contexts, Melanesian and Euro-American—indeed there are some radical differences[17]—but suggest how ideas can be borrowed across them. For it may help us appreciate people's interest in the intangible dimension of land to think of it as a kind of resource, bringing its own entitlements, analogous to the Euro-American notion of intellectual property.

Here we would be doing no more than countless people did during the 1990s UN Decade of indigenous Peoples. Country after country, under impetus from WIPO, UNESCO, with a sideways kick from TRIPS,[18] looked into the issue of protecting indigenous rights, including rights to indigenous knowledge and cultural resources, and looked to intellectual property rights (IPR) regimes as a model. By and large they have not kept *to* it as a model, but it was under the stimulus of thinking about IPR that many countries have considered developing regulations for the protection of culture and heritage.[19]

The leap of imagination is required, nonetheless, insofar as in Western jurisprudence land is often held up in *contrast* to intellectual property as the example of something that is manifestly tangible.

The second imaginativc leap requires an awareness of doing two things at once. We might suppose that anything that belongs to the realm of ideas has an infinite latitude—all the imaginings, poetic, artistic, scientific, there have been about landscapes come to mind—but I intend to ponder on how the intangible may be imagined as a *resource* (which is what intellectual property law is all about) and thus a part of what people have at their disposal in organizing and thinking about their lives. The notion of an intangible resource points to what might be at stake in claims that are incomprehensible when land is understood simply as a material or tangible one. For land can be both at the same time.

If it is useful to think of land as simultaneously a tangible and an intangible resource, then clearly these dimensions coexist. To see land as both means we *look at one thing and see another.* I use the visual metaphor because making things visible is an important vehicle of knowledge for the people I am talking about. In the context of a discussion (as this lecture is) it requires an imaginative leap.

Of course the ability to look at one thing and see another, that is, something that cannot be seen, is a common experience. The work of a recent Oxford graduate, Corsín Jiménez, anthropologist and geographer, is illuminating here. He has given us an account of an industrial mining city—set down in a desert in Chile—that is seen as unhealthy, dirty, and dangerous. When people look at litter they see delinquency, they look at graffiti and see vandalism, at the pigeons and see parasites. It is against this that they value their one tree-lined avenue with its provision of children's playgrounds, a destination for middle-class Sunday outings. And what do these city dwellers see? They see the clean esplanade and the swings and slides, and new shopping mall. But they *also* see themselves in a transformed state. As one resident put it: 'The kids love it, and it has changed the way families now spend their Sunday mornings. Before, one had to keep coming up with ideas of things to do to keep the children busy. Now people no longer feel so oppressed, so peripheral and neglected. Thanks to [the shopping mall] we are all a bit more central.'[20]

The anthropologist adds to this account. People do not just imagine themselves in certain ways. They make an association between places and forms of social relationships. They are able to 'get out' and 'do things', and that means being with family and friends. It means being able to be proper parents and do things with their children. They move through a space that they experience as a series of events with other people—going on swings, having tea, visiting the amusement park, enjoying a family outing.

So what has this got to do with the topic? The perceptions of city dwellers that seem far from any preoccupation with land—indeed the anthropologist-geographer was interested in their ideas of space precisely because they had nothing to do with territory—are not in fact alien to those who become concerned with land rights. It is just that in much of the developed world land is tied up in legal frameworks in a way that means it does not figure as the kind of issue it does in many developing countries. Yet that does not mean to say there are not continuities in the way we all think: looking at one thing, seeing another is a general human capacity. At the same time, there are discontinuities. I suspect that a perceptual education of sorts—acquiring double vision—is probably a prerequisite to understanding how passionate people become in matters of land. We might need to train ourselves a little to see things through other people's eyes.

Imagining Land

Looking at one thing and seeing another is a lesson that Papua New Guineans have taught many anthropologists.

Some time ago (but the story is still relevant) a small troupe of dancers from the New Guinea Highlands visited London. They had been taken round the metropolis, stood at the bottom of tall buildings, been herded across traffic crossings, experienced the vibration of vehicles pounding up and down, gone through steely glassy doors—the lot. They were not unused to these things, given Port Moresby, but the scale took them a back a little. At any rate, when asked how they found London they were polite; the trees are magnificent they said, really tall and flourishing! The trees? Of course.[21] Clearly London is wealthy and everyone knows that ultimately wealth comes from the land. But why the trees? Because they provide evidence of how good the land is. The land may be covered by buildings that are signs of wealth, but you can glimpse the land itself in the trees that also grow up from it, signs of its fecundity.[22]

Trees are not just evidence of the soil. They are also valuable in their own right. London was obviously largely cleared of woodland in order to flourish the way it did, and no doubt the timber was realized as an asset along the way. But if these people from the Highlands of Papua New Guinea were thinking about the land London was built on, back at home they would have added another dimension. For the land would flourish not just through how it was cultivated, but because of its association with specific ancestors who had worked the area and who were thought still to exert a benign influence. In other words it would have on it the 'name' of a particular group, a clan or lineage. The rights people had to enjoy the fruits of the land would depend on their entitlement through their links to the clan and its former members.[23]

We could think of that name[24] as a little like a trademark,[25] at least insofar as it is a name to which exploits are attributed and reputation accrues. It is simultaneously attached to the land and to those living there who walk around with its name on them, and engage with others in the name of the clan. Entitlement to use the name of the clan, regard oneself as a member, is restricted. But if it has analogies to property then Euro-American law would make a radical difference here. The timber, like the land it has come from, is tangible, 'real' as in real estate. It is possible to have possession of such items. By contrast, trademarks are primarily, as the lawyers would say, 'things in action': rights that can only be enforced by legal action as opposed to rights of possession. They belong to that class of property, intellectual property, generally described as *in*tangible.[26] Of course such property takes material form, but what is protected by the rights is the creative effort or (as here) image and reputation that is manifested in these forms. Thus copyright law exists to prevent others from taking advantage of one's creative activity. It must have a material expression, say as a particular text, but as a text, not as the printed page or the book. Similarly patent law can only be applied to artefacts, to things made, but what is protected is the right of the inventor to prevent others from exploiting without permission the original combination of ideas, knowledge, and effort that led to the invention.

Now in the New Guinea Highlands land that yields the staple food, sweet potato, is also divided up into territories; these are the notional spaces of clan groups. Look at the fallow bush and cultivated gardens and you also see something else: the ancestral dwelling place of this or that group. Its boundaries are marked, and protected. Of course it is not the hedges and ditches that people are protecting, it is their notion of the integrity of the clan that resides there. So one might call a boundary a piece of intellectual property: although it is not protected by a legal system, it is certainly a thing-in-action insofar as the rights to establish a boundary can only be perpetuated through people defending or activating it, that is, by the clan acting in its full territorial extent. This might echo the need to keep up claims to possession—a clan member has to activate particular claims to particular gardens by gardening there or loses them—but what is at stake is the intangible concept of the clan and its name.

From time to time the clan can make itself visible, although it will have to take a particular form to do so. It may be as a dance troupe or body of raiders attacking another group, or people lining up to vote in an election. But every such manifestation falls short of what the clan is in its totality.[27] For the clan endures as the generations of people who have lived on the land, and will do, who in their entirety can never be made visible. But it is displayed in a limited form on occasions when the clan comes together for a ceremony of one kind or another. In fact what is deliberately made visible or kept hidden for these people constitutes a technique for managing the relationship between the tangible and intangible. One can look at a set of dancers, and see in them the clan and generations of clansmen. Or one can look at an empty ceremonial ground and see the men and women who might have gathered there for an occasion.

Land in Extension

I have been talking about land as territory rather than as a horticultural resource that nurtures people and everything that grows on it, but in either case we could call the land productive.

For territory produces people too, only here they are people of a particular kind,[28] that is, it produces people with a specific name and identity. It produces social groups. Conversely, one can look at the clan and see its land, especially when the land is thought of as enduring over the generations. In this sense the most tangible landscape, one that the clan can possess, can also become a notional and intangible counterpart to the living body of people. However, this is the moment at which to question the concept of productivity.

First, what lies behind the notion of productivity? One could illustrate the Euro-American *productive model* from countless sources; here is just one. I choose it because it uses an analogy similar to the one I have deployed in suggesting we compare land to intellectual property. Here is intellectual property being compared to land!

It belongs to early formulations in England, at the time in the eighteenth century when a new notion was growing that authorial copyright could refer not just to the material but to the immaterial, not just to the book as a physical body but to a more abstract entity, the composition as a text.[29] Now simultaneously pressed into the authors' cause was an old equation between literary property and landed estates from which a living might be made. This was an idiom that authors borrowed from stationers (printers and booksellers). The latter had long argued that their copies (property that was at once the manuscript and the right to multiply copies of a particular title) were the equivalent of other people's estates. The Company of Stationers' petition of 1643 pleads that 'there is no reason apparent why the production of the Brain should not be as assignable [sellable] . . . as the right of any Goods or Chattells'.[30] While in the early modern period the most common metaphor employed to represent the author's relation to his writing is paternity (the author as begetter and the book as child), others included the author as singing shepherd, vessel of divine inspiration, magician . . . and tiller of the soil.[31]

In this metaphor, the image of land is being used to make the effort of intellectual work seem real or tangible. So what it introduces is the notion of the *produce* to be gained from the land. With that sense of tilling or harvesting comes also of course the idea of work, and the idea that the justification for property rights lies in the person's investment of *labour*. In other words people get produce from the land by dint of some exertion applied to it. That early modern logic still lingers. It departs radically from the Melanesian ideas I am dealing with.

Suppose we were in a world where no such value was put on labour? Where the entitlement to produce came from the entitlement to the land rather than from entitlement to the work? Where in fact when people speak of 'work' they mean the work of social relationships, the work of making connections, of tending to one another, and where the work of the hands is evidence of the way people keep their relationships in order? A person toils in the field for their parents or for their husband or child. Feeding the family from the fruits of one's own labour is an obligation that comes from relationships: a husband has a right to fruits of his wife's labour because they are married. But he also has a right because of his relationship to his clan and the generations before him who worked the land. So in this context we find that one intangible right demarcates another. Knowledge of relationships quite as much as memory of who occupied what places is the basis of claims.[32] Only thus can someone show that it is his—and in the Papua New Guinea Highlands I mean his not her—land on which the food is grown. And that goes for everything that the land grows, including livestock (pigs) fed off it.

These are, I suggest, not elements of a productive model of people's relation to land but of a *creative model*. I illustrate this in a moment. Meanwhile, note that entitlement to what the land grows comes from the entitlement to the land rather than entitlement to the work: for the land that creates the people creates in parallel everything else it yields. Trees, crops, pigs, and so forth. These are all to some extent analogous creations.

And if the entitlement to produce comes from an initial entitlement to the land, then we should see these creations not as an extension of people's labour but *as an extension of the land itself.*

What the land grows belongs to it; at the same time these creations may be detached and traded or consumed or otherwise disposed of. I have said that land is both tangible and intangible: I now need to introduce a distinction between the land that stays and the land that moves.[33] The land that stays is the enduring clan entity, the territory, the intangible and indefinite reference point for people's activities, and the continuity of persons who replace one another (as in a clan group). The land that moves are the people who travel back and forth, incoming spouses, the food that it grows, the pigs fed off it, and all the tangible items it is possible to possess in some way. These creations are, we might say, tangible forms or expressions of its intangible creativity. There is a distinction, then, between the land and its extensions, between land as creative and its extensions as creations.

All this can be summed up in the story that coastal people tell. In the central Highlands the enduring connection to the land is through ties through men; here, on parts of the coast, it is women through whom relationships to the land are stressed. The story is from Gawa island.[34] It is about the origin of canoes.

A group of men went to build a canoe. They hacked out a long hollow from the soil and tried to make a prowboard from rocks. They worked for months, years. One of their sisters got tired of cooking for the unending work and went to see how far they had got When the men showed her the hollow in the ground, she said 'What canoe is this? You are hollowing the soil!' She indicated[35] a tree growing from the land: that is what they should be building with. So canoes are made from the fruits of the soil, trees that can be cut down and carried away, and indeed canoes are vehicles for travel, trade, and exchange, and essential to the prestige men gain from their exploits overseas.

The moral of the story is that some things are appropriately cut and some not.[36] People should not appropriate the basis of life, of reproduction. The woman was saying, 'Don't try to extract what is creative: enhance your reputation through taking its creations.'

The land's creations are consumable or transferable extensions of land which itself, the source of creativity, is non-consumable and non-transferable. The guarantee of both possibilities—conserving the land and exploiting the fruits of the land—lie in the social relationships that are evidence of the way land owns people and people own land. To say that sweet potatoes or pigs can be regarded as an extension of the land, rather than of the cultivater who sweats to plant or tend them, is to say that they belong to the relationships in which that person is enmeshed. These are all particular relationships, and it is through particular relationships that people gain their personal reputations.[37] Incidentally, this gives us the rules of exclusion. No one else should take the planter's crop because the cultivation enacts the planter's, and not someone else's, relationships to others.[38]

Creations are at once specific extensions of specific, named areas of land, and detachable from them. So they flow across social contexts. *People mobilize both values at the same time.* And may make this visible. Thus they may use the vehicle of creations to point to the creativity of their land, and use the creativity of the land to point to the personal regard that comes to them from their own creations and accomplishments.

Visible and Invisible

But why do I say this is a *creative* model? It is partly to make a link with intellectual property rights that in turn make credible the idea that one can have property in the effects of creativity. The creativity of land in these Melanesian views exists as an intangible resource, made manifest in tangible objects—the creations—that can be transacted with and disposed of. It is partly to suggest that what people value is the intangible but vital *capacity for relationships* that the land and its fruits mobilize. But it is also partly to resonate with Melanesian ideas that connect creation and procreation. Here as an illustration I go back not to the seventeenth or eighteenth centuries but to the early twentieth century and what we know of the exploits of people of the Trobriand Islands, from the same region as Gawa. I do so because this is now history to present-day Trobrianders, and will be what they themselves have in mind when they recall the past.

These days people who once lived only on the Trobriand Islands off the coast of Papua New Guinea find themselves in Australia, America, and in the Papua New Guinea capital, Port Moresby, among the political elite.[39] National civil servants and company employees, they have to carve time out of other pursuits in order to maintain their gardens. Here they try to grow familiar root crops, the most prized root crop being the tuber, yam. In fact some have occasionally gone so far as to mount displays of urban creations like the harvest competitions people hold at home.[40]

The First Annual Trobriand Yam Festival in 1985 was supported by diverse bureaucrats and administrative officers.[41] It was to be an imaginative re-placing of the Trobriands in Port Moresby in order to show off the prowess of the Moresby residents. At home, displays of yam-growing test a gardener's capacity to turn his effort to effect in its impact on others. Now this effect requires a temporal distinction between a past period of time and the present moment. The period when yams increase in size and number in the ground is not simply assumed to be distinct from the moment when they are harvested and displayed: the two moments must be *kept* distinct. What is the significance of this? It is that by virtue of having happened already, the past activity is thus emphatically categorized as off-stage (hidden), and what happens off-stage is growth. This is land in its creative capacity.

What Trobriand gardeners themselves conceal for the moment is *their* harnessing of the land's capacity to increase the tubers *they* have planted in the ground. The analogy with the child in the womb would in the past have been explicit in magical spells accompanying the work; the yam is the gardener's 'child'.[42] Trobrianders make an equation between the fertility of yams and of persons, one constantly re-imagined through the competitive nature of harvest displays. For here yams are used as a measure of men's accomplishments.

Men confront other men with their displays, testing their respective capacities. Techniques of measurement make possible that imaginative leap from a gardener's expansive sense of effort to appreciating the material results of that effort. In the old days, one way of settling a dispute would be through competition, yams being displayed in special crates. However, the regular shows of yams intended for a man's sister and sister's husband or for the households of chiefs, were also measured, for they contributed to the augmentation and expansion of relationships.

Let me give a little of the detail to indicate the lengths to which people go to sustain the staging of their values. Each gift of yams was first assembled in the form of a cone near the garden site. The conical stack has to be composed in one go, a manoeuvre demanding a fine judgement of dimension and in particular of the size of the base.[43] The builder must project the correct dimensions for the base from the number and shapes of the tubers to make a stable and comely form. Its extent is recorded, with a length of rope, in terms of the circumference of the base. The stack is then disassembled, and the yams put into measuring baskets before being transferred to the storehouse of the recipient where they will be almost invisibly stacked away. The stores remain visible; the tubers inside hidden.

A tally is kept of the number of measuring baskets a cone has filled, the tally being displayed to the recipient when the stack is reassembled.[44] In competitive displays, after recording the individual contributions, men of a village amalgamate their yams. Individual stacks of exceptional size might reach 2,000 baskets; the bulk of one competitive harvest in 1918 yielded 20,000.[45] Yet whether on the Trobriands or in Moresby, the quantity of yams will only indicate prestige if they first indicate the power of the gardener. Like land, persons have inner capacities. In this sense persons, creations of the land, are also themselves creators.

Now a capacity that is only effective when it is hidden has to have an outward sign to make its presence tangible. The timing of events effects this. Very simply, as we have seen, two temporal moments (concealment and revelation) are kept distinct from one another. The activity being celebrated is categorized as off-stage, the time when things grow, but once the growing is complete the yam-children can be seen, and indeed *must* be seen (those on the outside of the stack may have their outsides painted). In addition is the question of the identity of the gardener: one has to be certain that the yams come out of the creator's own body, including its exertions, and not someone else's. That period of visibility lasts only for as long as the transactions take place: then the yams are hidden again.

The Moresby events that unfolded in 1985 raised problems for the city dwellers. In setting up the competition, they had wanted to make evident both their innate creative capacity and their personal prestige; personal prestige becomes in this sense a visible extension of that inner creative capacity. The men would achieve renown that would get back to the people at home, despite the work they had in Moresby wrestling the yams from its poor soils. But they could not keep the distinction between creativity and creations stable. According to Debbora Battaglia (see n. 40), both spacing and timing went awry.

Fundamentally, the men were unable to make the cones of yams next to their own gardens, and thus amass the tubers as they emerged from the ground. For fear of theft, they relocated them in residential areas. So instead of exposing the crop to view as it was harvested, they hid the yams again, packing them carefully to prevent damage in transit, and transporting the now invisible tubers in cars and pickup trucks across the city. This increase in distance became a hazard. Gardeners fell under suspicion for surreptitiously adding tubers from other sources, combining their own produce with other people's on the way. As a result, displays were growing at a time when growth ought to have ceased.[46] All this raised questions about whose creativity was being measured anyway, about who was entitled to make claims to having grown the yams. Criticism was levelled both at individuals and at the event as a whole.[47]

In sum, people are able to empower themselves at certain, usually ceremonialized, moments by playing on the relationship between intangible creativity and tangible creations. Thus they may turn the invisible creativity of the land into personal and highly visible *and* tangible power tokens for themselves (the yams at the moment when they are fed into relationships), and simultaneously may turn the visible creations of the land into invisible and in essence intangible resources (the yams hidden away in the stores).[48] Nothing could be more tangible than the baskets of yams: they are converted through storage into virtually invisible evidence of the strength of relationships of various kinds, and thus into the intangible prestige of the owner. Those yam houses are the standing record of the recipient's relationships with many others.

What Kinds of Rights?

Now the distinction between the creative capacity that land (and people) have within and the creations that, like the Gawan tree, can be detached and used in all kinds of exploits, primarily wealth-creation in this part of the world, is absolute. That is, it is held in place by protocols of all kinds. Its collapse in the case just given was potentially calamitous for everyone's reputation. Separately, each can be an index of—can point to the presence of—the other.

If land is creative and if its fruits or creations are regarded as extensions of it, then it is not too far off the idioms that many Melanesians deploy to say that such fruits are like bodies that come from bodies (the body of the land).[49] In other words, what flows from an inner quality comes outside. The idea that land *holds within* all kinds of potential, as yet invisible, value is what drives notions of land rights in present-day Papua New Guinea. Conversely, people compute the value of land by what is made visible. And these days the revenues from new forms of exploitation are very visible indeed. Here people's expectations are bound up with those of the Papua New Guinea state.

The country earns millions of kina (the national currency, in 1995 there being roughly four and a half kina to the pound sterling) from timber leases and mining and oil royalties. Some land is inevitably appropriated, but what people also have their eye on is the profits that will accrue to the company concerned. Profits spring of course from the continuing exploitation of resources. In fact in Papua New Guinea we see a consciousness of land rights most acutely expressed in terms of monetary demands.

Notably, these often take a very specific form that falls under the broad head 'compensation'.[50] Whereas shares in royalty payments exercise claims on new wealth, compensation is meant to redeem loss or damage suffered. K5 per hectare basic occupation fee; K15,000 per hectare for unimproved bush; K35,000 per hectare for land under cultivation; K520,000 for loss of 40 hectares of forested land, all as part of a payout of K35 million over half a decade. These are figures quoted for what is called 'land compensation', administered under the Papua New Guinea Mining Act, paid out for land absorbed into the operations of a gold mine in the Highlands.[51] The very concept of 'compensation' has a new resonance, and the Pidgin (Neo-Melanesian) term *kompensesen* covers a wider range of payments than former categories did. It tends to be used for any situation where people feel they have lost something to another person or been injured by them.

Now the sums people seek often seem exorbitant to the developers. In a series of law suits that began in the mid 1990s, a group of some 7,500 people living in the vicinity of the Fly River and the Ok Tedi mine claimed $2 billion Australian for compensation and A$2 billion as exemplary damages. (More than a 1,000 new writs were being filed in the National Court against the company and the government who between then held the major shares.) In the end a total settlement package of A$550 million was agreed.[52] It is hard to know what is exorbitant, however, when one learns that the mine has been dumping 80,000 tonnes of tailings *every day* into the 10,000 km long river system, creating a 40 km corridor of deforested and buried land from which life has long departed, and putting 3,800 sq km under threat of flooding. The pollution from suspended sediments and heavy metals in the river system has been estimated not as ten times or twenty times but as 10,000 times greater than American Environmental Protection standards would allow. The effects are visible all around.

Yet there is something about claims for compensation that puzzles observers, nationals, and non-nationals alike. There are continued complaints about the kinds of demands as, for example, faced the new University of Goroka with shutdown if the former landowners' bill for K4 million could not be met.[53] These have carried over from the success of getting compensation for land resources. For here what the profit-making developers complain about is that demands are set only by what nationals imagine the developers can pay. The new landowners are accused of scaling-up their demands according to the company's perceived wealth.

The nub of the matter is that *what commands a price indicates a resource*. Look at the money—the creation giving evidence of a tangible value—and see the intangible inner creativity of the land. Witnessing the inroads of foreign commercial ventures, of which the most obvious are land-based mining and logging, it is precisely the thought of company profit that prompts people to construe the counter-idea of recompense. In short, if fertility is a hidden quantity until it is revealed, it follows that anything that the land yields—oil, timber, gold—can be taken as evidence of inner resources. No wonder the new landowners do not pitch their price according to some pre-conceived value of the land but measure their demands against the developers' revenues.

There is a postscript here. I said that the term *kompensesen* can be used for any situation where people feel injury or loss, and we have heard how visible that can be when the land is damaged. But claims may also be made on other people when they have profited from one's own creativity. Now people profit from the creativity of others all the time; when that appropriation is embedded in the tie between them, given mutual acknowledgement, then it is greeted as part of the constant enhancing of relations. Such a view also covers bestowing creativity on generations to come. These days Papua New Guineans talk openly about the consequences of present decisions over land exploitation for the future of their children. And here they are talking about an intangible aspect of land very significant to them. This is precisely the power it gives them to expand and augment their relationships with others. They may in effect be demanding compensation for loss of that capacity, entailed as it is in loss of the sources of creativity whose creations they can no longer claim as their own.

The ideas I have been presenting lie at a tangent to much anthropological writing on land rights, although they echo issues in the way people conceptualize relations found in many places. Specifically, they have been prompted by the form of Melanesians' engagement with land. This has enabled me to try to convey a dimension to interests in land that is not exhausted by the concept of property rights in the Western (Euro-American) legal sense, until, that is, one thinks about intellectual property. I have tried to summon the intangible nature of people's claims through appeal to the general proclivity to look at one thing and see another. This is actually worked up to an art in this part of the world (Melanesia), since people there play on the way the visibility of one thing acts as a cue or index for things that are not visible. The observation brings me to two conclusions.

First, although what I have been talking about may summon far-off times and places there are significant continuities with what we may find anywhere. I have been at pains to stress this: fundamental to the notion of human rights is the presumption not just of common interests but of common ways of being in the world. At the same time, seeing through other eyes, putting oneself in another's shoes, whether in Chile or Berlin or on the Trobriand Islands, means realizing that the common world does not exist in a single dimension. We all have the capacity to look at one thing and see another. What we have to *enquire about* is just what that 'another' is in people's imaginations.

For, second, there are also radical discontinuities in the way we describe the world to ourselves. In classic Euro-American property law the distinction between the tangible and intangible was foundational, demarcating whole legal arenas.[54] It certainly demarcated the difference between entitlements based on the productivity of human labour and entitlements based on intellectual activity. But in a context where people make great play with what is or is not visible,[55] the distinction becomes blurred. What we find in its stead is a firm line between what one protects as the enduring resources of land, basically its creative potential, and its creations that are transactable. And there is a little more to it than a contrast between immovable and movable property. What is interesting about this part of the world (Melanesia) is the explicit way in which either can indeed be an index for the other, for the fruits of the land are regarded as an extension of it, that is, as land existing in another form.

Now this means that these people can refer in the same breath, so to speak, to *what is collective and what is personal.* They can simultaneously value the land for its creative and enduring potential, and they can strive to enlarge their own reputations and wealth through deploying its assets. In fact they do both these things at the same time. And this is where some of the confusions about land rights sometimes lie. Putting the contrast into the Euro-American language of individual versus communal rights, it sounds for all the world as though these people were both acting like individualists and like members of communities. Confusing indeed. For Euro-Americans that too—the individual versus the communal—marks a huge divide in property-thinking. Indeed in the 1990s the apparently 'communal' nature of many indigenous claims to cultural expressions was a prime reason for the ultimate failure of analogies with intellectual property regimes, resting as those did on the identification of individual authors and inventors.

Here we have come then to the very *starting point* of all those debates over land that pit individual rights against those of a communal or societal, or planetary, nature. The one seems diminished but precise, the other enlarged but diffuse. I hope this discussion will have served as a kind of introduction to the debates that follow, and as a reminder at least that it is possible to envisage at one and the same time people as owners of land and the land as owners of people.[56]

Response to Marilyn Strathern, 'Land: Intangible or Tangible Property?'

Laura Rival

Marilyn Strathern chose to introduce the Oxford Amnesty Lectures 2005 on land rights with a critical analysis of property as conceptualized in Western legal thinking, particularly the propensity of Western law to differentiate authors and owners of property, as well as its obsession with keeping individual claims separate from collective ones.[1] Melanesian people, she explained, see land as a resource that produces resources. This is why they do not divorce ownership from creativity. To them, the wealth-creating potential of land, that is, its productivity or creativity, derives from the double-sidedness of rights. If people own land, the reverse is also true: land owns people. This understanding of what ties people to land may be particularly Melanesian. However, the 'double vision', as she called it, is not specifically 'pre-industrial'. Everywhere, Strathern argued, legitimacy of wealth production, or, more precisely, property as the basis for profit, derives from land-owning-the-people rights as much as from people-owning-the-land ones. The language of rights is too narrowly focused on appropriation, on what is legitimate, and what is not. Moreover, legal categories artificially separate tangible from intangible property. As a result, Euro-American legal experts and lay people are equally prone to miss the remarkable similarities (and some of the striking differences) existing between cultures. From a rationalist and a humanist perspective, she concluded, the land rights of indigenous peoples (or of any other kind of people, for that matter) need not be argued on the basis of some mystical, primordial attachment to the land. Rather, what we need to do, and this is where a reflexive anthropology has an important role to play, is to elucidate the meaning of sociality, that is, the forms, articulations, and effects of social relations that underpin ownership.

I found much to admire in the lecture, and some conclusions worthy of debate. The first case examined by our lecturer concerned the clash between the Ok Tedi miners' right to pollute and the local population's right to subsistence. Analysed through the anthropological lens, the famous litigation case brings to light the Melanesian construction of land as a form of property which is at once material and immaterial, hence both sacred and exploitable. Melanesian people view logging and mining as good and legitimate activities as long as these render wealth visible. The mine's owners are not seen as creating wealth through the mobilization of human labour. Rather, they are seen to transform wealth that is already there, in the land. And the land belongs to the Melanesians. It is thus possible for the landowners to calculate the wealth hidden in their land and claim a share of it, especially once its inner productivity has been revealed by those who have developed it economically. Melanesian landowners compute the value of their land on the basis of the wealth rendered visible through exploitation, and not on the basis of an abstract measure of what is fair and just in compensation. This is why they have progressively adjusted their demands according to their perception of the company's wealth and profit making. In the Melanesian perspective, therefore, it is the creative work of perception which potentially generates new wealth.

The Melanesian way of creating new wealth through perception is further elucidated in the next example, which takes us on a tour of London with a group of visitors from Papua New Guinea. In the latter's 'double vision' (land owning people and people owning land), the city's immense wealth is understood to be hidden in the soil, and made visible, not in its imposing buildings, but in its vigorous, thriving trees. In their eyes, the trees lining the streets of London reveal the fertility of the land, that is, the real, inner, source of creativity. Fertility remains a hidden quantity until it is revealed by human labour, but the capacity to produce wealth is in the land itself.

This fact is further elaborated in the ensuing discussion of individual and corporate notions of ownership and belonging. For a Melanesian, but also for any one of us in a way, the power to produce is the power to materialize the 'mental' quality attributed to the land and to reveal it as visible wealth. Where the Melanesian and the Euro-American understandings diverge, however, is in the definition of what can be transacted or not. For the former, and clearly not for the latter, while the products of wealth creation capabilities are transferable and exchangeable, the capacity of land to generate wealth is held corporatively and exclusively by the clan.

Melanesians do not separate the personal from the collective. At once communist and individualist, if one may say, they mobilize the twin values of land as private and common in a way that is not open to us. For Strathern, one of the main problems with the legal language is that it reflects too much Euro-American obsession with bifurcating what is communal and what is individual.[2]

By contrast, the Melanesian property rights system recognizes the capacity of land to generate wealth as a common good, an inalienable possession, a creation that cannot be separated from procreation, as the next example illustrates so well. All Melanesian revelatory ceremonies involve a process of transformation in which the hidden wealth creation potential of the land is made visible. Trobriand annual yam festivals are archetypical in this respect. However, when city-dwelling Trobrianders attempted to organize a yam festival in their neighbourhood in the mid-1980s, they came to realize that traditional yam displays could not be sustained in the urban context, where they lost their meaning and value. They realized that in the city the connections between the fertility of yams and persons could no longer be made visible in a transparent manner. The ceremonial display failed to reveal the links between the invisible fertility of the land and the gardener's potency. Consequently, the process of transformation got short-circuited and open to suspicion.

In using these ethnographic examples, Marilyn Strathern hopes to lead us to re-think critically what ownership means in our culture. To fight against our built-in habits of thought, particularly those arising from our legal culture, we must consider property rights in their totality. She reminds us that definitions of ownership range broadly from belonging to exclusion of possession, and from primordial claim on the products of creativity to exclusive right of disposal. Mental and manual work are not separable from each other, and all forms of property are at once ideal and material, even the most material of all, land for instance. Not unlike the Physiocrats, she thus proposes that wealth ultimately takes its source in the land. However, her understanding of the value of human labour, informed by her long ethnographic acquaintance with Melanesian thought and her career-long interest in gender and property could not be further apart from theirs. Melanesians contrast rights to a land regarded as a source of creativity, and rights to its creation. Their understanding of property as the basis for profit is underpinned by a hybrid notion of land tenure as containing both tangible and intangible elements, material values and aspirations. Like Radin, who has judiciously remarked (after Marx) that 'property has made us so stupid and one-sided that we think a thing is only ours when we have it',[3] Strathern thinks that our laws define interests too narrowly. We are not fundamentally different from the Melanesians, but we tend to forget that land ownership is always a form of double belonging: we belong to the land as much as the land belongs to us.

What, for me, is missing in this critical rethinking of land rights is a historical and political reflection on why is it that our property laws fail to recognize that land as a source of creativity is often thought of, more, *lived as*, collectively owned, that is, protected from exclusionary claims. Whereas Strathern chooses to focus her critical effort on the illusory separation between the tangible and the intangible, or the visible and the invisible, I prefer to emphasize the relative power that land rights give to individuals and groups. The dominant Western jural[4] construction of property, entitlements, and what is legally transactable or not is highly contested, and has been so for a very long time, at least as long as struggles against social inequality have existed. A brief mention of anthropological work on property, land, and natural resources will suffice to illustrate this point.

For instance, in his seminal article on ownership and political ecology, Eric Wolf has already examined situations where the short-range interests of households were seen to run counter to regulatory controls of the community.[5] The ownership conflicts studied by Wolf arise at the intersection of narrow interests and broader ones, and they oppose short-term, productive decisions to collective decisions aimed at securing social reproduction in the long term. In his 2004 memorial lecture, Benedict Anderson[6] analysed ethnic conflict and violence in Indonesia as resulting from the clash between the inclusionary logic of citizenship and the exclusionary logic of common law property. He explained that for nationalism to succeed as a powerful ideology, the national territory had to be treated as a sacred space removed from the commodity process. However, with the rise of the middle class and the acceleration of resource competition, new private and common property rights emerge, which threaten the absolute rights of citizenship within national boundaries. Anderson stressed the fact that under capitalism common property cannot exist along private property as a form of property *of a different nature*. In my research on community forestry in lowland South America, I have similarly found a re-interpretation of communal land tenure regimes in terms of efficiency and transaction costs, and their ideological transformation into corporate ownership rights systems. Anderson concluded his lecture with an analysis of the transformation of common property into corporate property as a key exacerbating factor in the building up of ethnic tensions in South-East Asia.

I draw my third anthropological example from a recent paper by Frederique Apffel-Marglin,[7] which deconstructs the 'shyzophrenic logic' behind the massive land privatization movement occurring in the world today. Her critique of contemporary Western 'material realism' has some affinity with the critique developed by Marilyn Strathern in her

Amnesty International Lecture, and, like her, she searches for an alternative humanist approach to reality, which she calls 'agential realism', after the work of Karen Barad.[8] However, Apffel-Marglin radically departs from Strathern in her historical appreciation of the commodification logic that underpins material realism. Historically, the birth of material realism, she argues, embodied a new politics of commodification, and, in particular, the enclosure of commons lands. Not only did the enclosure of commons lead to the creation of labour as commodity, but it also triggered a new, depersonalized, relationship with nature. The gentry created themselves as exclusive owners of the commons, and forged new links between market incentives and their enclosed lands. These new links, essential to their power and legitimization, allowed them to disguise land appropriation as land improvements, and present wealth-hoarding and evasion of social responsibilities as progress. Because 'the commons was the privileged locus where rituals of gift exchange with the other-than-humans took place', their transformation into private property further promoted the separation of matter and spirit, and the rise of exclusive, calculative, modes of valuation. As the economy became an independent domain of value with its own laws, economic decisions were now divorced from their consequences, and the critical link between action and responsibility cut.

These three examples, no matter how briefly outlined, perfectly illustrate Strathern's point that the double belonging of land to people and people to land feed the human passions to defend rights and claims, for, ultimately, wealth continues to come from the land. But is it passions that are leading people 'to look at one thing, and see another'? For Strathern, whose recent work on cultural and biological ownership interrogates property definitions as matters of dispute over cultural form, the 'property relation' poses issues in complexity and scale. In order to discover what property relations make visible and what they obscure, she analyses legal frameworks as ways of turning words into action.[9] The problem with turning words into action, as she sees it, is that 'what may be important politically may be less than useful analytically'.[10] True, but to analyse disputes over property primarily as disputes over cultural form rather than over access and control has its own analytical limitations. What we need to theorize, I wish to contend, is the fact that land has creative potential, that is as potential resulting in creations that are transactable, is subject to multiple and overlapping claims of ownership. Moreover, the social actors who make these claims are not economically or politically equal. As Gregory illustrates so vividly in his remarkable study of land ownership in Bastar District (India), the regenerative capacity that ties kin together, and people to land, does not have the same meaning for the powerful and the powerless. Furthermore, and drawing on Gudeman's masterly redefinition of the economy as composed of two realms[11] to make this point, ownership as a relationship to the world is not one project, but *two*, according to where it is articulated, whether in the 'base' or in the 'market'. So in response to Strathern's comment that property rights can only apply to nature altered by human activity (remember it is human labour that reveals the inner wealth contained in the land), Gudeman and Gregory would answer that there are qualitatively different ways of altering nature, and they give rise to fundamentally different property rights regimes, which are used to distinguish regimes of incommensurable value.

2

Indigenous Peoples and International Human Rights

Romeo Saganash

At the outset, I would like to emphasize three preliminary points. First, when indigenous people speak of 'land rights', we generally refer to the broader context of lands, territories, and resources. For example, in regard to my own people—the James Bay Cree people—our traditional territory Eeyou Istchee includes lands, waters, and resources, and is approximately 400,000 sq km (about three times the size of England). It extends beyond the boundaries of the province of Québec and includes offshore islands and waters in James Bay and Hudson's Bay.

For thousands of years, the Cree people have occupied, governed, used, protected, and managed traditional territory. We continue to do so in a spirit of sharing. At the same time, we have a profound relationship with our territory and its resources and environment. This relationship has economic, social, cultural, spiritual, and political dimensions. Therefore, it is in this wide-ranging perspective that our 'land rights' must be considered.

Second, it is critical to appreciate the magnitude of the human rights challenges that indigenous peoples face today. There are over 300 million indigenous people in the different regions of the world. This includes more than 5,000 cultures. Yet we share a common legacy of human rights violations that still profoundly affects most indigenous peoples and individuals today.

The historical and contemporary experiences of indigenous peoples globally are most often described in such terms as dispossession, colonization and colonialism, racism and discrimination, exclusion, marginalization, cultural genocide or ethnocide, and genocide. These tragic and often brutal encounters with states, settlers, corporations, religious orders and other outsiders have resulted in far-reaching adverse impacts.

I am highlighting this global situation because it remains extremely urgent. Yet too often indigenous peoples are compelled to suffer abuses by states or others in virtual silence. Too often, within our various states, we simply do not have a voice. As I will later illustrate, in the human rights standard-setting process concerning indigenous peoples at the United Nations, there are a number of so-called democratic states that participate, but show little regard for these ongoing atrocities or other rights violations.

Third, in order to appreciate the various dimensions of indigenous peoples' rights to lands, territories, and resources, it is necessary to examine the broader context of our international human rights. This is because issues that we consider to be essential are viewed by some states as 'impediments' to making progress on the draft UN Declaration on the Rights of indigenous Peoples that is being considered in Geneva.

These key matters include: i) affirmation of our legal status as 'peoples' or 'indigenous peoples'; ii) affirmation of the right of indigenous peoples to self-determination *under international law*; and iii) affirmation of our collective rights as *human rights*.

All of these aspects are interrelated with the central issue of our land, territorial and resource rights.

The UN Standard-Setting Process: Background

In discussing the international human rights of indigenous peoples, it is vital to provide a brief background on developments within the United Nations. Human rights atrocities, both past and present, have compelled indigenous peoples to seek effective remedies outside the states or territories in which they live.

Since the early 1920s, the search for justice has brought indigenous leaders, representatives, and organizations to the United Nations or to its predecessor, the League of Nations. Over the past 20 years, I have seen indigenous people from different parts of the world—who had little or no means and had never before left their remote villages—find their way to the United Nations in Geneva. Many came in desperation and as a last resort.

Finally, in 1982, the UN took a significant step in responding to the growing global concerns of indigenous peoples. The Working Group on indigenous Populations (WGIP) was mandated to devote special attention to the evolution of standards relating to the rights of indigenous peoples. In 1985, the WGIP decided to begin work on a 'draft declaration on indigenous rights' for eventual submission to and adoption by the General Assembly.

During a period of about nine years, a draft UN Declaration on the Rights of indigenous Peoples was carefully formulated and ultimately approved by the expert members of the WGIP. Within this democratic and dynamic process, indigenous peoples, states, specialized agencies and academics actively participated and exchanged views. In 1994, the Sub-Commission on the Promotion and Protection of Human Rights (as it is now called) approved the draft Declaration elaborated by the WGIP and submitted it for consideration to the Commission on Human Rights (UNCHR).

While these achievements within the UN system generated much-needed optimism in regard to our human rights, a new reality was soon to appear. In the next stage of the standard-setting process, states and not independent international human rights experts would play a central and controlling role.

In March 1995, the Commission on Human Rights established an open-ended inter-sessional working group (WGDD) of the Commission on Human Rights with the sole purpose of elaborating a draft declaration. During the past 10 years, the WGDD has considered the text of the draft Declaration that was approved by the Sub-Commission and has made little progress in reaching consensus.

Only 2 of the 45 Articles in the draft *UN Declaration* have been provisionally approved by the participating states. The two Articles of the draft UN Declaration that were approved in 1997 only affirm individual rights. As a result, no text has been recommended for adoption by the General Assembly. Thus, at the end of the International Decade of the World's indigenous People in December 2004, its 'major objective' to adopt such a Declaration was not achieved.

The Grand Council of the Crees wholeheartedly commends the UN General Assembly for proclaiming a Second Decade to deal with indigenous issues at international level. This Second Decade, which commenced on 1 January 2005, can provide sorely needed opportunities to constructively confront the numerous challenges and problems facing indigenous peoples. However, the fate of the WGDD will only be determined in April 2005. At that time, the Commission on Human Rights will decide if it will extend the mandate of the Working Group and for what period.

At this point, it would be beneficial to pose two fundamental questions. First, why is it that international human rights experts, at two different levels of the UN system, were able to approve the whole text of the draft UN Declaration—which predominantly deals with the collective human rights of indigenous peoples? And, second, why is it that the WGDD during the past 10 years only approved 2 out of 45 Articles—which 2 Articles only affirm existing individual human rights?

In our respectful view and that of numerous other indigenous and non-indigenous organizations, the lack of progress in the WGDD can be attributed to at least two recurring and interrelated problems. One is a *lack of political will* among certain states and the other is the *discriminatory positions* being taken by them.

In considering these problems and the international human rights of indigenous peoples, I will devote particular attention to the positions of the United Kingdom, among other states. As will be demonstrated, the UK positions are highly inflexible, regressive, and discriminatory. They serve to severely impair the integrity of indigenous peoples' basic rights. If adopted, these positions could have widespread impacts on our status, rights, legal systems, and worldviews.

International duties to respect and promote human rights

In the context of the UN standard-setting process, indigenous peoples globally have repeatedly emphasized that the human rights norms in the draft UN Declaration must be consistent with international law and its progressive development. In striving to ensure that our fundamental rights are clearly embraced by the international human rights system, we have repeatedly underlined the duties of the UN and Member states to uphold the Purposes and Principles of the UN Charter.

As the UN Charter makes clear, its Purposes and Principles require actions 'promoting and encouraging respect' for human rights and not undermining them. The duty to promote respect for human rights is to be based on 'respect for the principle of equal rights and self-determination of peoples'.

Clearly, the UN and its Member states have no authority to weaken our human rights under international law and thereby create a double standard. In relation to both indigenous peoples and individuals, the creation of discriminatory double standards based on race would be a violation of international law, including the Purposes and Principles of the UN Charter. It would also be a violation of the peremptory norm that prohibits racial discrimination.

Thus, states could not validly agree to create discriminatory norms in a new Declaration on the rights of indigenous peoples or other UN instruments. Clearly, in such a situation, the obligations of member states under the UN Charter would prevail over those in any other international agreement. In regard to the *Charter* or other international instruments, legal obligations must be fulfilled in good faith.

In light of these essential principles and duties, it is most disconcerting and wholly unacceptable that some states in the WGDD are refusing to recognize that the collective rights of indigenous peoples are international human rights. Among others, these states include the United Kingdom, France, United States, Netherlands, Belgium, and Greece.

In its *Human Rights: Annual Report* of 2004, the UK Foreign and Commonwealth Office (FCO) states the government's position on collective rights in the following terms:

> With the exception of the right to self-determination, [. . .] we do not accept the concept of collective rights. *Human rights obligations* [. . .] *developed over the last half century require states to treat individuals, rather than groups of people, in accordance with international standards.* The key is that indigenous people should be able to realize their individual rights and participate effectively in decision-making processes, particularly on issues concerning land and resources.

In response to the UK's positions on our collective rights, indigenous organizations and nations from different parts of the world jointly submitted to Prime Minister Blair a 166-page analysis. This in-depth, substantiated Submission challenged the soundness of the presumptions and conclusions of the UK positions. Our overall conclusion is that the UK positions are in many ways discriminatory and that they cannot be sustained.

In direct contradiction to the UK positions, the collective rights of indigenous peoples are recognized as part of international law. For example, in the indigenous and Tribal Peoples Convention, 1989, reference is made to the human rights of the '[indigenous and tribal] peoples concerned'. It is only when the Convention specifically addresses the rights of individuals that the term 'members' of the peoples concerned is used. This Convention explicitly addresses various collective human rights of indigenous peoples, including land and resource rights. Under this Convention, state governments, with the participation of indigenous peoples, have a general legal duty to 'protect the rights of these peoples and to guarantee respect for their integrity'.

In addition, in such general instruments as the international Convention on the Elimination of All Forms of Racial Discrimination, the rights of 'groups' are explicitly contemplated. In the 1948 Genocide Convention, groups have the collective human right not to be subjected to genocide. In UNESCO's 1982 Declaration on Race and Racial Prejudice, it is underlined: 'The State has prime responsibility for ensuring human rights and fundamental freedoms on an entirely equal footing in dignity and rights for all individuals and *all groups*.'

Also, in what is commonly known as the Human Rights Defenders' Declaration of 1999, the UN General Assembly refers to the 'effective elimination of all violations of human rights and fundamental freedoms of *peoples* and individuals'. This includes systematic violations such as those resulting from apartheid, all forms of racial discrimination, colonialism, and the refusal to recognize the right of peoples to self-determination and the right of every people to exercise full sovereignty over its wealth and natural resources.

Further, the Inter-American Commission on Human Rights has interpreted existing human rights instruments to include the collective rights of indigenous peoples. A Working Group of Experts of the African Commission on Human and Peoples' Rights has also concluded that the collective rights of indigenous peoples are human rights.

It is especially noteworthy that, in 2000, the UK and other EU states entered into the 'Cotonou Agreement' with the African, Caribbean, and Pacific Group of states (ACP). Many of the 78 states that are currently in the ACP Group include indigenous peoples. In this legally binding international agreement, it is stated:

The Parties refer to their international obligations and commitments concerning respect for human rights. *They reiterate their deep attachment to human dignity and human rights, which are legitimate aspirations of individuals and peoples.* Human rights are universal, indivisible and inter-related. *The Parties undertake to promote and protect all fundamental freedoms and human rights,* be they civil and political, or economic, social and cultural.

Yet it would appear that, in relation to indigenous peoples, the UK and other opposing states remain oblivious to all of these human rights obligations, commitments, and realities. To date, we have never received a substantiated response to the specific human rights arguments that we have raised in our analyses or in our discussions in Geneva.

Instead, in defence of its positions, the UK has called on a number of erroneous arguments that are replete with discrimination. These arguments are generating confusion and division. They include the following:

- First, *that treaties entered into prior to 1948 have no relevance to international human rights law.* However, this view has been contradicted by the Inter-American Commission on Human Rights. The Commission has recently concluded that, in regard to human rights issues pertaining to indigenous peoples, it was necessary to review their particular historical context as well as relevant treaties, legislation and jurisprudence that developed over more than 80 years.
- Second, *that collective rights are 'granted' or given by national governments and, therefore, must be kept separate from international human rights law, which deals with individual rights.* However, the Supreme Court of Canada has ruled repeatedly that the collective Aboriginal rights of Aboriginal peoples are 'inherent' or 'pre-existing'. The existence of our collective rights

is not dependent on any recognition or 'grant' by national governments. Aboriginal title to land has been determined to 'arise from the prior occupation of Canada by Aboriginal peoples'. Moreover, a diverse range of international bodies address indigenous peoples' rights in the context of human rights.

- Third, *that the draft UN Declaration seeks to 'create' new collective rights specific to indigenous peoples*. However, this view is contradicted in the draft *Declaration* itself, which refers to the 'inherent rights . . . of indigenous peoples, especially their rights to their lands, territories and resources'. In addition, the British government entered into numerous historical treaties with indigenous peoples which affirmed their collective rights. For example, the Treaty of Waitangi, entered into with the Maori in 1840, explicitly affirms their collective rights.
- Fourth, *that collective rights are a threat to the individual human rights of indigenous persons*. For the UK to pre-judge all collective rights in such a stereotypical manner is highly discriminatory and ignorant. Equal recognition of the collective human rights of 'peoples' cannot, in itself, be a violation of the rights of 'individuals'. Indigenous individuals often exercise rights that flow from our collective rights. Recently, the UK contradicted its own position by expressly conceding that the collective rights of indigenous peoples are 'crucial to the very existence and integrity of indigenous peoples as distinct peoples, and provide the political, social, economic and cultural context within which indigenous people can best enjoy their human rights'. However, to repeat, the UK does not regard these collective rights as human rights.
- And fifth, *that individual human rights must always prevail over collective rights*. However, this prejudicial assumption

would not allow for possible balancing to occur between collective and individual rights that should be based on the particular facts in any given case. In any human rights dispute, should it arise, a 'contextual analysis' would take place based on the particular facts and law in a specific situation. This is the fair and just approach that is generally accepted under both international and domestic law.

Rights to Lands, Territories, and Resources: the Need for a Self-Determination Context

Let us now turn briefly to the right of self-determination and land-related issues.

Recognition and respect for the right of self-determination and other collective human rights establish an essential context for the enjoyment and exercise of indigenous peoples' rights to lands, territories, and resources. Without an adequate land and resource base, the impoverishment of indigenous peoples by states and others will continue. In addition, the survival and well-being of distinct indigenous peoples and the integrity of our nations, communities, cultures and legal systems will be severely jeopardized.

Since the collective human right of self-determination is specifically included in both international human rights Covenants, one would expect that states participating in the WGDD would apply this central right on an equal basis to indigenous peoples. After all, each and every state that has ratified at least one of the Covenants has an affirmative legal obligation to 'promote the realization of the right of self-determination, and [...] respect that right, in conformity with the provisions of the Charter of the United Nations'.

Yet many of the states in the WGDD, including the UK, United States, France, the Netherlands, and Australia, are still not willing to fulfill these legal obligations. They still refuse to affirm unequivocally that the right of 'all peoples' to self-determination in Article 1 of the Covenants applies equally to indigenous and non-indigenous peoples. In the case of the UK, Secretary of State Hilary Benn has acknowledged that 'The fact that many indigenous peoples are anthropological "peoples" is clear, and is a vital part of their identity.' Curiously, he qualifies this by adding 'It is not generally accepted as a matter of international law that the right of self-determination in common Article 1 applies to indigenous peoples per se'.

This latter position fails to respect the interpretations and conclusions of the treaty-monitoring bodies, such as the UN Human Rights Committee and the Committee on Economic, Social, and Cultural Rights. Both these bodies have applied Article 1 of the Covenants to indigenous peoples, including the rights to natural resources. Consistent with the right of self-determination under international law, the Committee on the Elimination of Racial Discrimination has repeatedly stated that indigenous peoples have the 'right to own, develop, control and use their communal lands, territories and resources'.

With regard to indigenous peoples, the Committee on the Rights of the Child has explicitly endorsed the self-determining approach of these three treaty-monitoring bodies. In terms of improving the conditions affecting Aboriginal children in Canada, the Committee has explicitly highlighted the importance of the observations and recommendations on lands and resources by these bodies.

It is worth noting that the Human Rights Committee is using the collective right of indigenous peoples to self-determination as a normative standard to interpret individual rights under the Covenant. Therefore, any state that seeks to deny or otherwise undermine the recognition of the right of indigenous peoples to self-determination—including the right to natural resources—is also impairing the full and just recognition of the human rights of indigenous individuals.

In contrast to these positive developments within the UN, UK representatives at the WGDD have suggested creating a 'new right' of self-determination in the draft UN Declaration that would apply globally to indigenous peoples. According to its latest position, the UK would restrict this right to internal self-government. This unjust approach and position is exceedingly difficult to comprehend. On the one hand, the UK insists—albeit erroneously—that the draft UN Declaration must not create new rights, specific to indigenous peoples. On the other hand, the same government shies away from the existing right of all peoples to self-determination in the human rights Covenants and proposes to create a new right for indigenous peoples.

The UK delegation in Geneva has repeatedly registered its objection to the use of the term 'peoples' throughout the draft Declaration. The UK intends to retain this objection, until it is satisfied that the collective rights associated with the term 'peoples' in the Declaration are fully excluded or segregated from the international human rights system. However, in international law, the status of indigenous peoples as 'peoples' is a matter of fact. It is not a question that is dependent on the arbitrary discretion or political choice of states.

For states to deny indigenous peoples the status of 'peoples' in order to deny them the right of self-determination would be clearly discriminatory. It would be contrary to both the International Convention on the Elimination of All Forms of Racial Discrimination and the International Covenant on Civil and Political Rights. Yet the UK and certain other states continue to maintain their positions on self-determination with remarkable impunity.

In my respectful view, these double standards are inappropriately linked to the UK's refusal to fully apply the right of self-determination *under international law* to indigenous peoples without discrimination. This has far-reaching adverse implications for our rights to lands, territories, and resources.

'Individualizing' the Collective Rights of Indigenous Peoples: a Destructive Alternative

The UK and other state governments are in effect offering indigenous peoples a choice: either accept that indigenous peoples' rights are really individual rights that may be exercised collectively, 'in community with others', or these states will continue to oppose any affirmation that our collective rights are human rights. These attempts by states to individualize indigenous peoples' rights directly contradict the rulings of domestic courts and international human rights bodies. In particular, our rights and titles to lands have been repeatedly confirmed to constitute the collective rights of indigenous peoples or nations.

In Article 1 of the international human rights Covenants, it is explicitly highlighted that the right of all peoples to self-determination includes economic, social, cultural, and political dimensions. As elaborated in the draft UN Declaration, our fundamental rights are also clearly of an economic, social, cultural, and political nature. These same classes of rights are addressed in the two international human rights Covenants. In relation to indigenous peoples, these types of rights cannot suddenly lose their human rights quality simply because of their crucial collective dimensions.

To restrict international human rights to individual rights would only serve to assimilate or otherwise undermine our cultures, traditions, legal systems, and world views. It would run counter to the basic principles of diversity, tolerance, and equality—all of which embrace the right to be different. It would also negate a key reason for adopting a UN Declaration on the Rights of indigenous Peoples.

We have already described to the UK and other like-minded states the far-ranging adverse effects of individualizing our collective rights. For example, in the United States, 90 million acres of Indian land were lost, after the US government unilaterally adopted the General Allotment Act of 1887 and divided tribal lands into small parcels and allocated them to individual Indians and non-Indians. As recently described by the US Bureau of Indian Affairs, this 'policy was a failure' and has shattered the integrity of many indigenous territories with ongoing destructive impacts.

In New Zealand, since the nineteenth century, Maori customary rights to land and their land regime have been converted to an Anglo-Saxon type of regime. As a result, almost none of the customary lands are left. The majority of these lands have become acquired private property, most often by the Pakeha, that is New Zealanders of European origin. Similarly, a Working Group of Experts of the African Commission on Human and Peoples' Rights has recently cautioned:

> Policies of individuation of tenure are continuing in Kenya and this has in many cases had disastrous effects for the pastoralists, especially

the Maasai, who have ended up losing the land that is crucial for sustaining their livelihood and many now find themselves completely impoverished.

Whether some states continue to seek to individualize our collective rights or strive to exclude them from the international human rights system, these misguided actions cannot be justified by the principle of universality of human rights. To a large degree, universality is a flexible concept that embraces the human rights of all peoples and individuals.

The draft UN Declaration, which focuses primarily on collective rights, is intended to apply *universally* to all indigenous peoples in all regions of the world. In some ways, this is also similar to other human rights instruments that apply universally to all women, or to all children, or to all persons with disabilities, among others, so as to better achieve equality and enjoy their human rights. Human rights instruments do not have to apply to everyone in exactly the same way. Rather, the principle of equality accommodates or otherwise includes the 'right to be different'. In order to achieve equality, different peoples or people often have to be treated differently.

As confirmed in the 1993 Vienna Declaration, the principle of universality of human rights accommodates 'national and regional particularities' and historical and cultural differences. This is wholly consistent with the imperative of cultural diversity, which is inseparable from the human dignity of peoples. All cultures form part of the common heritage of humankind and we will continue to contribute to this ongoing legacy from our own distinct perspectives.

Our collective and individual human rights are interrelated and interdependent. They cannot be artificially separated, so that the individual rights dimensions are human rights and the collective rights aspects are excluded. Our human rights are wholly consistent with international human rights law. As the Vienna Declaration confirms: 'All human rights are universal, indivisible, interdependent and interrelated.'

We, as indigenous peoples, will not tailor our human rights to fit the latest assimilationist designs of self-serving states. As described by Grand Chief Ted Moses in November 2004: 'Current UK policies on indigenous peoples' human rights are relics of colonial policies that have failed.'

Concluding Remarks

In order to address effectively land, resources, and other key human rights issues of indigenous peoples, it is necessary to confront the matter of discrimination. As my lecture today illustrates, the widespread biases we face are not limited to the diverse domestic contexts within existing states. It is also evident in the standard-setting process relating to indigenous peoples' human rights within the United Nations.

Throughout history, indigenous peoples worldwide have been discriminated against in every way possible. We have been deprived of our lands, territories, and resources through so-called doctrines of dispossession—such as 'discovery' and *terra nullius*—and by labelling us as 'savages', 'heathens' or 'infidels'. For most of our history, indigenous land and resource rights did not qualify as property rights. Our traditional land tenure systems were *different* from non-indigenous systems and, therefore, our land and resource rights were unjustly deprived of equal recognition and protection.

We have also faced, and continue to face, profound systemic discrimination from some within the United Nations.

While wholly unacceptable and contrary to the UN Charter, this may have been foreseeable. Many of the same states that have profoundly discriminated against us in domestic contexts have willfully carried their same 'baggage' of biases with them to the United Nations.

For example, in order to deny indigenous peoples our rightful legal status as 'peoples', the WGIP that was created in 1982 is called the Working Group on indigenous Populations. Many states have always believed—and some still do—that if they deny the legal status of indigenous peoples, it will be easier to deny us our right to self-determination and other human rights.

This abhorrent rationale was the basis for not adding an 's' to the term 'people', when referring to indigenous peoples in the Vienna Declaration and Programme of Action in 1993. Such shameful actions were carried out by states, despite the vigorous protests of indigenous representatives at the World Conference on Human Rights and despite the fact that states were in the process of formulating and adopting a human rights instrument. This was also why no 's' was added when the UN General Assembly proclaimed the International Year of the World's indigenous People in 1993 or the International Decade of the World's indigenous People.

Similarly, upon the insistence of such states as the US and Canada, a paragraph was added to the indigenous and Tribal Peoples Convention, 1989 with the hope of limiting the meaning of the term 'peoples' in international law. However, the Chair of the International Labour Organization revision process indicated in the minutes of the proceedings that this issue was beyond the competence of the ILO. Therefore, a neutral position was maintained in relation to the Convention.

At the same time, we acknowledge with deep appreciation the many bodies within the UN and its specialized agencies that have refused to be a party to such overt racial discrimination. Clearly, their principled positions constitute the strong majority point of view within the UN system.

Should any of you choose to visit the web site of the UK's Foreign and Commonwealth Office (which is responsible for human rights issues), you will note that the FCO generally uses the term 'people' and not 'peoples' when referring to indigenous peoples. Apparently, the UK pays little attention to the Harare Commonwealth Declaration, 1991. This Declaration requires all Commonwealth members to 'recognise racial prejudice and intolerance as a dangerous sickness and a threat to healthy development'.

In order to address the consequences of racism and racial discrimination against indigenous peoples, it is vital to eliminate the deep-rooted prejudices exhibited by a number of states within the WGDD. Discriminatory state positions are likely the largest impediment to a successful conclusion in the standard-setting process.

In particular, proposals from the UK and other states to exclude or segregate the collective rights of indigenous peoples from the international human rights system should not be tolerated. Such a regressive step would severely blacken the reputation of the United Nations and its member states. It would be contrary to existing international human rights instruments, the conclusions and rulings of international human rights bodies, and international law as a whole.

It would severely undermine the integrity of our rights, cultures, and legal systems. It would create an inherent incoherency, namely that the indispensable collective rights of indigenous peoples, from which diverse individual human rights flow, are not in themselves human rights. states would feel emboldened to continue the condemned practice of 'extinguishing' indigenous peoples' collective rights, since these rights would purportedly not constitute human rights.

All states, including the UK, must fully respect the UN Charter and fundamental principles of justice, fairness, democracy, and respect for human rights. They must respect the rule of law, not only domestically but also at the international level.

Those states that refuse to recognize our collective rights as human rights are failing to respect the inherent dignity of indigenous peoples. Although indigenous peoples are distinct and equal 'members of the human family', our collective human rights are being disrespected and devalued. This reprehensible conduct constitutes a serious and ongoing violation of the most basic values and principles of international law. As UK Parliamentary Under Secretary Bill Rammell publicly declared in March 2004: . . . 'the opening words of the Universal Declaration on Human Rights . . . state that 'recognition of the inherent dignity and of equal and inalienable rights of all members of the human family is the foundation of freedom, justice and peace'. In other words, without the observance of human rights by all states, freedom, justice, and peace are fundamentally threatened.

The global geopolitical implications of the regressive and illegitimate positions being taken by the UK and certain other states in the WGDD transcend the indigenous context. As described and concluded by indigenous peoples:

> . . . in the current geo-political context . . . [t]he UN and its Member states are implementing a diverse range of measures internationally. These include promotion of international peace, security and

cooperation; combatting terrorism; prosecution of crimes against humanity; and addressing other issues of global concern.

states who selectively apply, or fail to comply with, the principles of democracy, rule of law, peace, justice, non-discrimination and respect for human rights can hardly demand full respect for these same precepts and values from other states.

On human rights issues, the lack of impartiality in the positions of the UK, U.S. and certain other states have grave implications that go far beyond the more than 300 million indigenous people in different regions of the globe. Selective or discriminatory application of the *Charter*'s Principles—whether by developed or developing states—substantially weakens the United Nations and the international human rights system as a whole.

In order to effect positive change, indigenous peoples have recommended specific reforms in the functioning of the WGDD. These include the introduction of explicit criteria within the Working Group, so as to ensure strict adherence to the Purposes and Principles of the UN Charter when any participant proposes new or modified human rights norms. In particular, proposals to undermine the human rights of indigenous peoples or create discriminatory double standards should not be afforded any credibility within the Working Group.

Too often, states fail to provide any substantiation for their positions or proposals. We need more effective checks and balances within the WGDD to address the erroneous and discriminatory arguments of some states.

States should be calling attention to proposals that would violate international human rights standards. The performance of state obligations is a legitimate interest of the international community. Consistent with democratic principles, human rights organizations and other human rights defenders in civil society also have an essential role.

Thus, ensuring the affirmation of and respect for indigenous peoples' human rights is not solely an indigenous responsibility. It is also a matter of international concern and cooperation. In terms of the overall strengthening of all human rights, there is too much at stake for all.

Response to Romeo Saganash, 'Indigenous Peoples and International, Human Rights'

Ellen L. Lutz

Throughout history, indigenous peoples have been among the most beleaguered and subjugated. They have survived genocide, disease, forced assimilation, exploitation by powerful economic interests, poorly considered development policies, and the negative consequences of globalization. In many parts of the world their marginalization is worsened by ethnically-dominant neighbours who deny their existence or are uncomfortable in their presence.

Since 1982, the United Nations human rights machinery has played a significant role in focusing world attention on the human rights violations indigenous peoples face, including abuses of their rights to their lands and resources, violations of their rights to cultural expression, and denials of their rights to be full and effective participants in the political processes that impact their lives. The United Nations also has played a leading role in strengthening protections for indigenous peoples' rights, and increasing the extent to which indigenous peoples and their cultures are respected and protected from neglect, discrimination, and abuse.

But a sea change has occurred with respect to international indigenous rights law since Romeo Saganash delivered his Oxford Amnesty Lecture on indigenous peoples and

International Human Rights in February 2005. After nearly a quarter-century of negotiation, on 29 June 2006, the newly formed United Nations Human Rights Council adopted a draft Declaration on the Rights of indigenous Peoples. That text has been forwarded to the United Nations General Assembly for final approval in December.

Even in its 'draft' state, the Declaration has been a beacon for indigenous peoples in their efforts to induce states to respect their autonomy, rights, and cultures. In many countries indigenous peoples have persuaded their governments to incorporate all or part of the draft Declaration into constitutional or national law. International and national courts have cited it as authority in determining the rights of indigenous peoples to territory, resources, and economic, social, or cultural rights. The Declaration is relied upon by international aid agencies, funders, and nongovernmental organizations as the standard to be applied with respect to indigenous peoples. Thus, it could be argued, the draft Declaration on the Rights of the World's indigenous Peoples has made an end-run around the normal processes of international law-making. It is normative. Much of it may be on its way to becoming customary international law, like the Universal Declaration on Human Rights.

Unlike most draft declarations, which are drafted by small groups of experts or UN bodies made up of member states, the draft Declaration on the Rights of indigenous Peoples emerged from a lengthy negotiated process between a UN body of experts and the world's indigenous peoples. While indigenous peoples are not recognized as 'sovereign states' as a matter of international law, they regard themselves as sovereign. The very purpose of the drafting process was to recognize and give definition to that sovereignty. The negotiation process was delicate because indigenous peoples are many and varied and do not share a common point of view. Yet in terms of their rights in relationship to states, a consensus emerged that balanced the self-determination needs of indigenous peoples with the realities of a world organized into sovereign states.

While the draft Declaration frequently is heralded for its comprehensiveness and sensitivity to indigenous concerns, what less often is appreciated is what the draft Declaration is *not*. Even after it is adopted by the UN General Assembly, the Declaration on the Rights of indigenous Peoples will be just that—a Declaration. Declarations like this one are regarded by jurists as definitive statements of UN members states' obligations under the United Nations Charter. They are frequently cited by governments, courts, or arbitral tribunals as evidence of customary international law. Often they form the basis for future treaties. But declarations are not treaties, and they are not offered to states to ratify and thereby bind themselves as a matter of international law. Nor do they create new enforcement machinery to which victims can turn if their rights are violated. Unless new mechanisms are created, political embarrassment is the only sanction states will suffer if they violate a declaration.

On the other hand, the more UN bodies and states embrace human rights declarations as normative and institutionalize mechanisms to ensure that they promote and protect the rights they contain, the greater their legal weight. Fortuitously, the opportunity to establish more reliable means to sway states to comply with the provisions of the Declaration on the Rights of indigenous Peoples is being presented by the restructuring of the UN's human rights machinery. The new Human Rights Council is directly accountable to the UN General Assembly. It is made up of states elected by the General Assembly from a pool of countries that have met threshold human rights criteria, and it is scheduled to meet regularly throughout the year. The aim is to avoid the pitfalls of the current Human Rights Commission which has long been bogged down by political infighting among states seeking to protect themselves from challenges to their own rights violating behaviour.

The challenge facing the new Human Rights Council is to build an international institution that has the capacity to motivate states to comply with current and future human rights norms—including those set forth in the Declaration on the Rights of indigenous Peoples.

Some might argue that indigenous peoples already have adequate voice within the United Nations through the UN Permanent Forum on indigenous Issues. But while enormously valuable, the Permanent Forum is a sub-body of the UN's Economic and Social Council (ECOSOC) and, as such, its mandate will remain focused on economic, social, and cultural development issues that range well beyond the compass of human rights enforcement. Because of its UN advisory and coordination role, it is not in a position to do human rights standard-setting or monitoring. Responsibility to ensure that indigenous peoples' rights are treated as a matter of high priority throughout the United Nations system lies with the new Human Rights Council.

This year, as the new Human Rights Council defines and institutionalizes its operating procedures, it should take the following four additional steps to ensure that indigenous voices are heard, and that violations of indigenous peoples' rights come promptly, and as a matter of priority, before the Council:

1) **Ensure that indigenous Peoples are Effectively Represented before the Human Rights Council**

Currently, indigenous Peoples are able to participate in United Nations human rights meetings that address indigenous rights without meeting all of ECOSOC's consultative status criteria. It is important that indigenous peoples not lose opportunities to give voice to their concerns within the United Nations. As new mechanisms for consultative status with the Human Rights Council are established, special consideration should be given to providing opportunities for indigenous peoples whose organizations are local, focused on topics other than or in addition to human rights issues, or have organizational structures that do not fit standard non-governmental organization models to participate.

2) **Establish an Advisory Body on indigenous Peoples' Rights**

The Human Rights Council should establish its own high level advisory body to advise it on human rights issues of concern to indigenous peoples. Examples of such advice might include mechanisms for reviewing the rights set forth in the Declaration on the Rights of indigenous peoples; thematic reports like those now being conducted by the Sub-Commission's Working Group on indigenous Populations; new normative instruments for the protection of indigenous peoples' rights; etc. It should have the same power to receive information from indigenous Peoples as the Sub-Commission's Working Group now has. In addition, it should have regular communication with the UN Permanent Forum on indigenous Issues. This body should be composed of both Council members and indigenous members.

3) **Include indigenous Rights as Part of the Universal Periodic Review**

In setting up the new system of universal periodic review of governments' human rights records, the Human Rights Council should ensure that indigenous peoples' rights are among the regular topics addressed. In addition, the Human Rights Council should invite indigenous peoples from the states under review to contribute their perspectives to the review process.

4) **Continue the Office of the Special Rapporteur on the Human Rights and Fundamental Freedoms of indigenous People**

This office is one of the most effective tools for promoting and protecting indigenous peoples' rights worldwide. Its mandate should be continued, and reinforced with greater support and funding, so that the Special Rapporteur can continue his vital case and country mission work, which has produced laudable results for indigenous peoples.

The Human Rights Council was not unanimous in adopting the draft Declaration. Some Council members, such as Canada, and some indigenous peoples and NGOs lobbied member states to postpone voting on the Declaration. They argued that because UN declarations are non-binding and depend on the good will of states for their implementation, it would be better to hammer out the remaining disagreements and then adopt it by consensus at a future meeting, rather than take a potentially divisive vote now. This view was rejected and, on the penultimate day of the session, the Council put the draft Declaration to a vote. Thirty states voted in favour. Two states—Canada and the Russian Federation-voted against it; twelve states abstained.

The United Kingdom, which Romeo Saganash singled out in his Oxford Amnesty Lecture for its regressive attitude towards the international legal rights of indigenous peoples, was one of the Council members to vote in favour of the draft Declaration. The UK government may have heard what Saganash had to say in Oxford last year, as its vote seems to meet him half way. In its explanation after the vote, the United Kingdom stated that it welcomed the Declaration as an important tool to enhance the promotion and protection of the rights of indigenous peoples, and regretted that consensus on it could not be obtained. Further, it asserted that its concerns had been addressed in the negotiations that led to the final draft, and that it fully supported the provisions of the Declaration that recognized the rights of indigenous peoples under international law, on an equal footing with all.[1]

But, as Saganash excoriated in 2005, the United Kingdom continued to insist that it did not accept the concept of collective rights in international law. Rather, it understood the right of self-determination as set out in the Declaration as one which was to be exercised within the territory of a state and which was not designed to impact in any way on the territorial integrity of states. It further underscored its view that the Declaration was not legally binding and that the citizens of the United Kingdom and its territories overseas did not fall within its scope.[2]

This undoubtedly is depressing news for the llois peoples of the Chagas archipelago in the British Indian Ocean Territory, the Tahitian descendents living on Pitcairn Island, and any Taino whose homelands are on Caribbean islands that are part of the United Kingdom. But it is a disturbing announcement in another way for it suggests that the UK negates the progressive development of international human rights law, particularly where that law applies to groups rather than individuals.

The significance of the Declaration on the Rights of indigenous Peoples lies in the fact that in addition to individual rights, it recognizes the collective rights of indigenous peoples. It normatively affirms existing international law, which Saganash comprehensively surveyed in his lecture, that where indigenous peoples are concerned, issues such as self-determination and land rights apply to the whole group, and can be addressed only at that level. State compliance with many of the draft Declaration's articles requires consultation with, participation by, and prior informed consent of indigenous peoples before decisions are taken.

At the close of the Human Rights Council session, UN Permanent Forum on indigenous Issues President Victoria Tauli Corpuz summed up the sentiments of the world's indigenous peoples when she stated,

> The real test will be how this will affect the lives of our people on a daily basis . . . While these are distinct and fundamental individual and collective human rights, it is their implementation at the community level, which will have an impact and give our children hope for a future where their lives and identity will be respected globally.'[3]

3

Standing in Deep Time; Standing in the Law: A Non-Indigenous Australian Perspective on Land Rights, Land Wrongs, and Self-Determination

Frank Brennan

Mr Rhodes, *Terra Nullius* and Contemporary Values

There is something passing strange about an Australian Catholic priest, descended from Irish immigrants, standing at a podium in Oxford in 2005 daring to offer an opinion on indigenous land rights and self-determination. What right do I have to speak? What could I usefully say? I take heart from Amnesty International's conviction that the ordinary person can make a difference by having a commitment to public advocacy and private communication with both the prisoner and the jailer, acting in solidarity with the prisoner and putting pressure on the jailer. As a non-indigenous advocate for indigenous rights, I am committed to dialogue with all parties and to public advocacy that keeps hope alive—the hope of finding common ground, sharing country and reconciling differences in societies whose indigenous members have survived the adverse effects of colonization.

Being a priest speaking about land rights on the cusp of old Europe, I am haunted by the words of Chief Justice Marshall in the 1823 decision of the US Supreme Court *Johnson* v *McIntosh*:[1]

On the discovery of this immense continent, the great nations of Europe were eager to appropriate to themselves so much of it as they could respectively acquire. Its vast extent offered an ample field to the ambition and enterprise of all; and the character and religion of its inhabitants afforded an apology for considering them as a people over whom the superior genius of Europe might claim an ascendancy. The potentates of the old world found no difficulty in convincing themselves, that they made ample compensation to the inhabitants of the new, by bestowing on them civilization and Christianity, in exchange for unlimited independence.

I have agreed to participate in this Oxford Amnesty Lecture series knowing that indigenous speakers have preceded me. In my home country I have been a long time advocate of Aboriginal land rights and self-determination. That has not spared me some spirited disagreement with Aboriginal representatives. And of course, government apologists see me as an incurable romantic dreaming of the noble savage's renaissance. Having been privileged over many years to participate in the indigenous struggle for land rights in my home country, I still believe in that struggle and the primacy of Aboriginal aspirations for self-determination while Aboriginal leaders seek to accommodate themselves to the realities of their traditional communities, the demands of government, and the expectations of the descendants of their colonizers.

Without land rights and self-determination, indigenous peoples in previously colonized societies are treated as the members of one polity without a voice and as people without distinctive rights. With land rights and self-determination they are members of two polities with their own conflicting voices (realist, liberal, and idealist), living under two laws which require reconciliation when the indigenous law and the colonizer's law collide or when the indigenous person asserts individual rights against the collective rights of the clan or community. Land rights and self-determination provide the space and the time for these indigenous peoples to live in their two worlds.

Indigenous people without land rights and without a modicum of self-determination are individuals and societies denied the place and opportunity to maintain themselves with their distinctive cultural identity in a post-colonial, globalized world. Indigenous people with land rights and a modicum of self-determination are individuals and societies with an enhanced choice about how to participate in the life of the nation state and of the global economy while being guaranteed the place and opportunity to maintain their cultural and religious identity with some protection from state interference and from involuntary assimilation into the predominant post-colonial society.

This evening I will argue four propositions about previously colonized societies with indigenous minorities:

1. Law and policy should recognize that even today indigenous minorities in these societies have to live in two worlds, and the common good of these societies (as well as respect for the rights of the indigenous citizens) requires some recognition of land rights and self-determination.

2. Indigenous leaders are like politicians dealing in international affairs. They have to deal with their domestic constituencies and treat with the leaders of other governments which happen to be the elected governments of all the people in the post-colonial society. As in the field of international relations, there will be indigenous leaders and theorists who are realists or idealists and others seeking reconciliation in the centre, who are liberals. All must be heard.

3. Indigenous people should be free to opt for their individual rights as citizens regardless of the arrangements between government and the indigenous leadership.

4. Only by tolerating the uncertainty and complexity of land rights and self-determination can non-indigenous people own their history and their responsibility for the continuing plight of their indigenous citizens.)

I think it appropriate in Oxford to commence discussion about land rights with reference to the Privy Council's 1919 decision *In re Southern Rhodesia* in which Mr Rhodes' British South Africa Company was a party. This decision related to land transactions between Cecil Rhodes and the natives of Zimbabwe which may in part have contributed to some of you being able to study here at Oxford, while the indigenous people suffered dispossession and deprivation. The other parties to the proceedings were the Legislative Council of Southern Rhodesia, the Crown, and the natives. Lord Sumner in his report of the Privy Council wrote:[2]

> By the disinterested liberality of persons in this country their Lordships had the advantage of hearing the case for the natives who were themselves incapable of urging, and perhaps unconscious of possessing, any case at all. Undoubtedly this inquiry has thereby been rendered more complete.

Leslie Scott KC and Stuart Bevan are described as appearing 'for the natives', perhaps the shortest and most generic description of a party ever to appear in the authorized law reports. On the next page of his Report, Lord Sumner writes:[3]

> The estimation of the rights of aboriginal tribes is always inherently difficult. Some tribes are so low in the scale of social organization

that their usages and conceptions of rights and duties are not to be reconciled with the institutions or the legal ideas of civilized society. Such a gulf cannot be bridged. It would be idle to impute to such people some shadow of the rights known to our law and then to transmute it into the substance of transferable rights of property as we know them.

Lord Sumner observed that there was 'a wide tract of much ethnological interest' between these tribes and other indigenous peoples 'whose legal conceptions, though differently developed, are hardly less precise than our own'. He thought the natives in question 'approximate rather to the lower than to the higher limit'.[4] According to the Privy Council, the maintenance of native title rights 'was fatally inconsistent with white settlement of the country' which 'was the object of the whole forward movement, pioneered by the Company and controlled by the Crown . . . with the result that the aboriginal system gave place to another prescribed by the Order in Council'. The Privy Council concluded its consideration of the native title claim, 'Whoever now owns the unalienated lands, the natives do not.'[5] The natives were the people of one new polity without a voice, under one new law without rights.

Turning to the dispute between the company and the Crown, the Privy Council decided that the British South Africa Company was entitled to dispose of any unalienated lands using the proceeds to offset the costs of administration. Should the crown terminate the Company's administration of Southern Rhodesia, the company was entitled to reimbursement from the Crown for previous costs—either from the proceeds of further land sales or from public funds.

At the height of colonial expansion by European empires, those indigenous groups who bore some resemblance to their colonial masters were to enjoy some recognition and protection. Those differing from their new masters who could barely comprehend their social reality were to be denied any semblance of land rights and self-determination. Such Eurocentric notions put blinkers on the law's horizons of justice.

Seventy-four years after the Privy Council's decision about the fortunes of the British South Africa Company, the High Court of Australia had, for the first time in the *Mabo* case, to consider the rights of the Australian 'natives' to the 'unalienated lands'. In 1992, that court decided to discard the distinction between inhabited colonies that were deemed to be *terra nullius* and those which were not:[6]

> If it were permissible in past centuries to keep the common law in step with international law, it is imperative in today's world that the common law should neither be nor be seen to be frozen in an age of racial discrimination.
>
> The fiction by which the rights and interests of indigenous inhabitants in land were treated as non-existent was justified by a policy which has no place in the contemporary law of this country.

With the removal of the blinkers used by Lord Sumner and most Europeans of his time, indigenous people are not guaranteed a better life, but they can be assured the legal and political preconditions for better participation in the life of the nation state, while maintaining and adapting their traditional places and lifestyle.

The contemporary Australian court went on to say:[7]

> Whatever the justification advanced in earlier days for refusing to recognize the rights and interests in land of the indigenous inhabitants of settled colonies, an unjust and discriminatory doctrine of that kind can no longer be accepted. The expectations of the

international community accord in this respect with the contemporary values of the Australian people.

Does this reference to contemporary values imply that the judges thought the majority of Australians, if asked in an opinion poll, 'Do you support aboriginal land rights?', would have answered unequivocally 'Yes'? I do not think it can mean that. I am prepared to accept that the majority of Australians if asked that question in 1992 would have answered 'No'. The values that underpin the *Mabo* decision are respect for property, the desire for certainty in the conduct of relations relating to land, predictability in the application of the law by courts for the resolution of conflict, and non-discrimination in the sense that governments should not treat persons differently unless there is a coherent rationale for such different treatment. In particular, governments should not treat more adversely people's property rights simply because they are members of a particular race. These are the enduring values of contemporary Australians.

After the *Mabo* decision, I met with the senior partners of one of Australia's largest legal firms. They were agnostic about the decision's effect, doubting that it had really changed anything. I pointed out that my line of work had not changed but that prior to *Mabo* it was called politics; post *Mabo* it was called law. It was unimaginable prior to *Mabo* that a Jesuit working for Aboriginal rights would have been invited to the annual retreat of a leading law firm. Something had changed.

At the end of the session, one of the lawyers, a Mr Murphy, pointing out that his ancestors were Irish, asked: 'If there are special rights for the Aborigines, why don't you have special rights for the Irish?' Being a Brennan and my mother an O'Hara, I have some sympathy for the rights of the Irish in

Ireland. I take some consolation and pride in the fact that there is somewhere on earth that the Irish can be as Irish as they like, with minimal interference by other persons. The more relevant comparison is not with the rights of the Irish in Australia but with the rights of the Irish in the Republic of Ireland. There is only one place on earth where Australian Aborigines have any prospect of living out the fullness of community lives as Aborigines. That is on the Australian continent, though as part of a nation state where as an indigenous minority, they will be far more circumscribed in their distinctive cultural choices. But there are possibilities for them, and those possibilities are enhanced by recognition of their land rights and their ongoing entitlement to self-determination within the life of the nation.

The Symbolism and Utility of Land Rights

Indigenous groups with some recognition of their land rights face the dilemma: how to live within the nation state participating in its economy while maintaining distinctive culture and heritage. That ought be their decision, and no one else's, even if that someone else be a government with a fresh political mandate. Those of us who are non-indigenous members of such nation states need to guarantee the minimum requirements for these indigenous groups to make a realistic choice. Doing so, we have the opportunity, at some considerable cost, to ground our national identity and project in the depth and complexity of the history of our land and all its peoples.

In 1995, I made my first trip to the United States. I headed directly to Alaska. On arrival at the St Mary's Yup'ik Eskimo community on the Andreafski River, a small tributary of the mighty Yukon, a local community member offered to show me around the community. Despite my jetlag, I readily agreed. I was keen to meet members of an indigenous community who were assured a significant degree of self-determination and land rights as far as the eye could see. This woman took me first to the local cemetery. I was perplexed. She told me the story of the lives and deaths of the three young men who had been most recently buried in the cemetery. She told me the story of the community without breaching the confidences or imposing on the privacy of any of the living. There were tales of violence, alcoholism, and dreadful accidents. The similarities with so many tales that I had heard on Aboriginal communities over the years were stark—and far more immediate than the legal and political differences that distinguished the land rights and self-determination of Alaskan and Australian communities.[8]

That night I was devastated as I reflected on what I had heard at the cemetery. One of the local Jesuits showed me a series of newspaper articles highlighting the dreadful social problems confronted by indigenous communities living close to the Yukon. But how could this be? These people had not only secure land title over their community lands but also other economic benefits flowing from the Alaska Native Claims Settlement Act of 1971. They had self-determination. They not only had their own law-making councils. They had their own courts and their own police; their own schools and a secure land base together with the economic security of a fishing resource which was seemingly boundless in that part of the world—all we could have dreamt of in Australia. And they lived in such a remote place that very few outsiders had an interest in living there or disturbing them. They had known Russian and American governments and prided themselves on maintaining their traditions and identity no matter which flag flew at the post office.

No matter which country you survey, no matter what that government's policy, no matter what the present strategy of indigenous leaders, and no matter what the public understanding or sympathy about the position of indigenous minorities, land rights for indigenous people are an essential component in providing indigenous citizens with the choice and the potential to live an authentic indigenous life within the realistic confines of nationality and economy. Land rights are also the cornerstone for the settlement of historic post-colonial grievances in:

- Providing a land base for some indigenous persons and communities
- Providing some indigenous communities with economic and political bargaining power, assuring them a place at the table
- Recognizing the entitlement of indigenous communities to maintain and sustain their religious beliefs and practices, without threatening the public order of the society after colonization
- Correcting some historic injustices which can be put right without occasioning injustice to other persons
- Validating the post-colonial legal system, providing a greater coincidence between law and justice
- Providing a necessary forum for the resolution of conflicting claims
- Assisting all citizens of the nation state to appreciate the place and entitlements of indigenous people
- Assisting all citizens of the nation state to reach a better understanding of their history and their place in the world

Australia is distinctive because our history of land rights is so brief, our approach so pragmatic and belated, and our commitment to land rights so refreshingly new, fragile, and wavering. While no one seriously suggests substantive change to the system of landholding for indigenous communities in New Zealand, Canada, or the United States, some Australians now entertain the hope or thought that Aboriginal problems could be solved if community land titles were transformed into alienable individual titles, encouraging indigenous communities to leave behind their traditional ways and enter the contemporary marketplace with an initial bonus of transferable land title.

You will recall that Captain Arthur Phillip arrived at Sydney Cove on 26 January 1788 and established a penal colony for undesirable persons from this part of the world, given the future unavailability of the American colonies which had revolted. The six Australian colonies were the only British colonies in which there was no recognition of land rights. Only in the last 35 years in Australia, land rights have been recognized for the first time, accepted as part of the just settlement, and now questioned as symbolic, wasteful, and misdirected policy. Land rights and self-determination are the stuff of 'culture wars' in Australia.

While everyone is in favour of reconciliation between indigenous and other Australians, protagonists distinguish practical reconciliation and symbolic reconciliation.[9] Conceding the legitimacy of past grievances, some now see land rights as a symbolic issue providing little practical assistance to Aborigines wanting to live contemporary lives, or even worse, as providing a dead-end panacea for life separated from the mainstream, in the backwater of community life without economic prospects or relief from the entrapment of the past. While land rights is seen by some supporters as an honouring of the Aboriginal spiritual relationship with land, others view land rights as a simple matter of setting right an historic injustice, or as a matter of economic empowerment. I was once asked by a publisher, 'Is land rights about power or culture?' I answered, 'Both', and still do.

Sir David Lange, ex-Prime Minister of New Zealand and renowned Oxford debater once gave the after-dinner speech at an Australian conference on indigenous and environmental issues. Lange was bemused by his trans-Tasman audience and told us: 'You Australians are always looking for the final answer to the Aboriginal question. There is no final answer. There are only durable solutions which can last a generation or two when once again you will have to sit down and negotiate an agreement for the future.' That is one reason why the more conservative Australian politicians have always opposed the idea of a modern treaty. It never gets to the stage that you can draw the line and put the past behind you. There will always be indigenous dissatisfaction because of the historic injustices and because of the ongoing marginalization which comes from being a minority in the society post-colonization. There is no definitive answer for those living in two polities under two laws.

Indigenous Claims to Land Rights in the *Terra Nullius* of Australia

At Yirrkala, Arnhem Land, in the Northern Territory, no penal colony had ever been established. The people there had traded regularly with the Macassans from Indonesia. A few Englishmen had come there attempting to run pastoral properties in the nineteenth century but they failed and moved on. In 1935, the first white men settled there. They were a couple of

Methodist missionaries and their families. Some Aborigines from Arnhem Land had visited Darwin and seen the conditions in which the Larrakeah people were living as fringe dwellers on the outskirts of town. They did not much like what they saw of white urban society and its treatment of their Larrakeah kinsmen. In 1963, the Commonwealth government excised 300 square kilometres from the Aboriginal reserve in Arnhem Land in preparation for the proposed granting of a 42 year lease to a Swiss consortium Nabalco for the mining of bauxite.

Some forms of mining are not very intrusive. Bauxite mining requires the stripping away of the entire land surface. Regeneration of the land takes many decades. Aborigines who had a long undisturbed and spiritual relationship with the land, celebrating ceremonies at sacred sites for which they cared, were very troubled to learn that a government in Canberra thousands of miles away could give permission to a foreign corporation to destroy their land, invade their community and upset their sacred sites. With the help of the Methodist missionaries, they sent back petitions in their own language and in English to the parliament in Canberra respectfully requesting that they be consulted about any measures impacting on their community or on their lands. The first petition concluded:

- That the people of this area fear that their needs and interests will be completely ignored as they have been ignored in the past, and they fear that the fate which has overtaken the Larrakeah tribe will overtake them.
- And they humbly pray that the Honourable the House of Representatives will appoint a Committee, accompanied by competent interpreters, to hear the views of the people of Yirrkala before permitting the excision of this land.

- They humbly pray that no arrangements be entered into with any company which will destroy the livelihood and independence of the Yirrkala people.
- And your petitioners as in duty bound will ever pray God to help you and us.

Then in 1966, the Gurindji people living at Watti Creek in the Northern Territory walked off Lord Vestey's cattle station demanding better wages and title to their traditional land. They were also concerned about the sexual exploitation of their women by white workers on the Vestey property. This 'walk-off' became one of the great emblematic events in Australian land rights. The leader of the walk-off, Vincent Lingiari, became the father figure of land rights. Nine years after the walk-off, Prime Minister Gough Whitlam went to Watti Creek, now known by its traditional name 'Dagaragu', to hand over a lease of the land to the traditional owners. Pouring a handful of earth into the hands of Vincent Lingiari, Whitlam spoke for the nation when he declared:

> Vincent Lingiari I solemnly hand to you these deeds as proof, in Australian law, that these lands belong to the Gurindji people and I put into your hands part of the earth itself as a sign that this land will be the possession of you and your children forever.

Lingiari replied, 'They took our country away from us, now they have brought it back ceremonially. We are all mates now.' The leaders of two polities had met and the voice of each was heard. This was a novel development in the *terra nullius* of Australia. Each leader spoke with authority for the land: two polities, two laws. Two song writers (Kevin Carmody, an Aboriginal, and Paul Kelly, a white Australian) wrote a song 'From Little Things Big Things Grow':

That was the story of Vincent Lingiari
But this is the story of something much more
How power and privilege can not move a people
Who know where they stand and stand in the law

Four years before the ceremony at Dagaragu, I had commenced my university studies. A student of politics and law, I was interested to hear Aboriginal protesters who came on campus demonstrating against the policies of the Queensland government on Aboriginal reserves. Like many white Australians, I had not previously heard Aborigines speak. I found it difficult to believe that there were places where Aborigines lived, managed by white public servants who controlled many aspects of Aboriginal life. I heard stories about the need for Aborigines to receive government approval to marry. Public servants could even dictate the style of swimming costume that could be worn. These communities had no right to their traditional lands and they were still paid minimal wages. Aboriginal voices were heard on the national airwaves. Aborigines were pleading their case with the people, with the parliaments, and finally in the courts.

Having received no satisfaction from the politicians after the lodging of their 1963 petitions, the Yirrkala Aborigines turned to the courts in 1968. Thus began one of the long games of legal and political ping-pong in which the cause of land rights went backwards and forwards between the courts and the parliaments, over the net of public opinion. Milirrpum and Mungurrawuy were the leaders of the two clan-owning groups, the Rirratjingu and the Gumatj clans. They were joined by Daymbalipu, the leader of the Djapu clan who had access to the Rirratjingu and Gumatj lands for hunting and foraging. Expert anthropologists, including W. E. H. Stanner, joined traditional Aboriginal owners in explaining the system of traditional Aboriginal law and the Aboriginal connections with land. The judge, Sir Richard Blackburn, was impressed but troubled. After considerable delay, he handed down his decision in 1971, which happened to be my first year of law studies. Justice Blackburn observed:[10]

> The evidence shows a subtle and elaborate system highly adapted to the country in which the people led their lives, which provided a stable order of society and was remarkably free from the vagaries of personal whim or influence. If ever a system could be called 'a government of laws, and not of men', it is that shown in the evidence before me.

However, he felt compelled to rule that the British common law did not recognize communal interests in land as described in the evidence in court. Even if it did, he ruled that all such interests would have been extinguished by the assertion of sovereignty by the British Crown. The lawyers for the traditional owners saw little point in appealing the case, even though these were disputed propositions of law, because the judge had also ruled against the Aborigines on the facts. He said, 'I am not satisfied, on the balance of probabilities, that the plaintiffs' predecessors had in 1788 the same links to the same areas of land as those which the plaintiffs now claim.'[11]

With no further recourse in the courts, the Aborigines looked again to the politicians. Change was in the air with the election of the Whitlam Labor government in 1972. That government was elected with a commitment to legislate for the recognition of Aboriginal land rights in the Northern Territory. After a royal commission, legislation was proposed and it was passed in amended form by the Australian Parliament at the instigation of the Liberal Country Party government led by Malcolm Fraser after the governor-general, Sir John Kerr, dismissed the Whitlam Labor government. Aboriginal traditional owners were granted inalienable title to their lands and a right to veto mining on their lands. The veto armed these owners with economic bargaining power. If they had the power to say 'No', they were able to say 'Yes, subject to conditions favourable to us.' The recognition of the Aboriginal spiritual relationship with land carried with it the prospect of economic enhancement.

Meanwhile Eddie Koiki Mabo, a Torres Strait Islander, was living on the Australian mainland, having been denied permission to return to his island homeland by Queensland public servants who thought him a troublemaker. He decided to organize the Meriam people, a group of Torres Strait Islanders from the Murray Islands, to bring a case in the High Court of Australia to challenge the findings of law made by Sir Richard Blackburn in the 1971 *Milirrpum* decision. He thought Blackburn got the law wrong. He also argued that even if the High Court agreed with Blackburn, the case of the Torres Strait Islanders was distinguishable from that of mainland Aborigines for two reasons. First, Torres Strait Islanders were not traditionally hunters and gatherers. They cultivated vegetable gardens and lived in huts in settled villages, thereby having individual interests in discrete blocks of land rather than communal interests in vast tracts of country. Second, the Queensland crown as sovereign had continued to recognize Torres Strait interests in land. The Queensland government had even set up courts to determine land disputes between islanders even though no land titles had been granted by the crown. Eddie Mabo had a passion for putting right an ancient wrong, and the imagination and bold vision to see it through to the highest court in the land. It is one of the tragic ironies of the law that Mabo, like the claimants in the original *Milirrpum* case, did not establish his own native title claim because the trial judge did not accept his evidence. However, his co-plaintiffs, including Father David Passi, did succeed. Mabo's action provided the vehicle for a declaration of native title by the nation's highest court.

The Queensland government's response to Mabo's claim was one of the last-ditch stands by governments still blinkered by the *terra nullius* mindset. The government introduced to the Queensland parliament the Queensland Coastal Islands Declaratory Bill of 1985. The bill was promptly passed. It was only 14 lines long. It deemed that Torres Strait Islanders did not have any rights to their traditional lands prior to the assertion of the Crown's sovereignty over the islands in 1879 or that alternatively all rights were extinguished retrospectively to 1879 with no compensation being payable. The government explained that this bill would avoid the need for limitless research work on mere matters of history being agitated in the courts. As the legislation was inconsistent with the Commonwealth Parliament's Racial Discrimination Act, the High Court struck down the Queensland provision in 1988, giving Eddie Mabo and his co-plaintiffs the much needed encouragement and opportunity to proceed with the substance of their case.[12] On 3 June 1992, the High Court of Australia declared that 'the Meriam people are entitled as against the whole world to possession, occupation, use and enjoyment of the lands of the Murray

Islands' and that the title of the Meriam people is subject to the power of the Parliament of Queensland and the power of the Governor in Council of Queensland to extinguish that title by valid exercise of their respective powers, provided any exercise of those powers is not inconsistent with the laws of the Commonwealth.[13]

As the sun rose over the tip of Cape York on 12 October 1993, the waters of the Torres Strait were exceedingly calm. As the sun glistened on the water, Father David Passi, the Anglican Pastor of the Island of Mer in the Murray Islands group, stood at the back of the speedboat pointing at a small island close to the shore, declaring, 'That's Possession Island.' David smiled broadly as he explained that this was the place where James Cook came ashore after his epic voyage up the Australian eastern coastline in 1770, raising his king's flag and claiming possession in His Majesty's name of all he had sailed passed. David chuckled, 'Cook had his back to the Torres Strait when he claimed possession.'

Next day at Bamaga on the tip of Cape York, David explained the significance of the *Mabo* decision to a meeting of his fellow Anglican clergy. His people believe that in ancient times a figure named Malo set down the law for relations between islanders regarding their lands and waters. All islanders speak of the myth of Malo-Bomai. Malo and his maternal uncle made a long sea journey from West New Guinea across to Mer in the east. These mythical heroes, Malo resembling an octopus, brought the eight peoples or clans into one, 'strengthening them with the qualities of a diversity of sea creatures, so giving the power to match the sea and make long journeys across Malo, the deep seas, for canoes and for battle.' In this part of Australia, the indigenous people define themselves in relation to land, sea, each other and seasonal time or prevailing wind.

Fr Passi, known also as Kebi Bala, explains Malo's law:

For thousands of years we have owned the land and Malo who was the Meriam centre of it made sure that members of the society were given land. They are our laws. We have Malo ra Gelar. It says that Malo keeps to his own place; Malo does not trespass in another man's property. Malo keeps his hands to himself. He does not touch what is not his. He does not permit his feet to carry him towards other men's property. His hands are not grasping. He holds them back. He does not wander from his path. He walks on tip-toe, silent and careful, leaving no signs to tell that this is the way he took.

Passi explains that since colonization there have been two laws, 'the white man's law and Malo's law'. Malo's law is respectful of people's history and connection with the land. The white man's law is strong. It believes might is right. Those who believe in Malo's law have to convince those who practise the white man's law that Malo's law is right. Might alone is not right. Speaking about two laws, David Passi was using the discourse of two polities and two religious traditions.

Even the most trenchant critic of the *Mabo* decision in the Australian Parliament, after travelling to the Torres Strait said, 'It is perfectly obvious to me that those people have owned that land forever as history has been recorded. But it is different to say that all over Australia we should have a feast for lawyers.'

The decision was basically a judicious realignment of the common law developed by judges to match the historical reality with the historic land grievance which for the first time had come before the highest court in the land. The decision posed no threat to sovereignty nor to the Treasury coffers. The decision was an honest acknowledgement that most Aborigines had been long dispossessed of their lands and any restitution or compensation was a matter for parliaments rather than the courts. The decision provided an historic opportunity to put right those wrongs of the past which could be put right and to acknowledge those wrongs which forever stained the nation's identity. This could be done without any threat to any other person's land rights or legitimate economic interests. The decision provided a unique opportunity for a negotiated settlement of the nation's longstanding land rights question with Aborigines at the government's negotiating table and holding some of their own trump cards.

Two centuries after European settlement, most Aborigines had been dispossessed of their lands. A just settlement of land grievances required more than the recognition of those rights that had escaped extinguishment by governments which had operated for generations with a *terra nullius* mindset. The Parliament set up a land fund for the purchase of lands on the open market for the benefit of those Aborigines who had lost their traditional lands.[14] There is now a National Native Title Tribunal with almost 600 applications pending, half of which are going through mediation. The government funds Aboriginal representative bodies which have their own advisers. Professor Marcia Langton says, 'What's become clear is that whereas litigation is costly and time consuming, agreement-making costs less and is more timely.'

There have been more High Court cases since *Mabo*.[15] Both the Labor and Liberal-National Party governments have tried their hands at legislative responses to the High Court's native title decisions. Paul Keating led the nation in espousing the correctness and decency of *Mabo*. John Howard told Parliament that *Mabo* 'now with the passage of time, seems completely unexceptionable to me. It appears to have been based on a good deal of logic and fairness and proper principle.'[16] The dust has settled. The decision is not seen as a revolution but as a belated common-sense piece of legal reasoning.

Initially the mining industry was very concerned that the recognition of native title could cause a massive slowdown in mining and exploration. On the tenth anniversary of the decision, Tim Shanahan, CEO, Chamber of Minerals and Energy (WA) said, 'Mining companies in the early days weren't as sanguine or accepting of native title. These days it's seen as part of the normal business of mining.'

The belated recognition of native title has helped to put right what two of the High Court justices described as our 'national legacy of unutterable shame'.[17] The High Court still has its work cut out interpreting the fine print of the excessively amended Native Title Act and filling in the detail of common law native title, providing considerable feasting for lawyers. Indigenous communities still have their problems and we still have a national problem in reconciling ourselves. The denial of land rights and the failure to accord equal protection and respect under the law are no longer part of the Australian solution. That is a better starting point than the *terra nullius* mindset which preceded *Mabo*.

Justice McHugh, who is the only judge who decided the *Mabo* case still sitting on the High Court, has had cause to look back over the history of native title litigation:[18]

> The dispossession of the Aboriginal peoples from their lands was a great wrong. Many people believe that those of us who are the beneficiaries of that wrong have a moral responsibility to redress it to the extent that it can be redressed. But it is becoming increasingly clear—to me, at all events—that redress can not be achieved by a

system that depends on evaluating the competing legal rights of landholders and native-title holders. The deck is stacked against the native-title holders whose fragile rights must give way to the superior rights of the landholders whenever the two classes of rights conflict. And it is a system that is costly and time-consuming. At present the chief beneficiaries of the system are the legal representatives of the parties. It may be that the time has come to think of abandoning the present system, a system that simply seeks to declare and enforce the legal rights of the parties, irrespective of their merits. A better system may be an arbitral system that declares what the rights of the parties *ought to be* according to the justice and circumstances of the individual case.

Other High Court judges have voiced similar concerns.[19] The issue now is not the legitimacy of land rights but determining the cut-off point for recognizing native title rights when other parties also have rights over the same land, and matching the remaining native title rights with the real, rather than imagined, Aboriginal and Torres Strait Islander aspirations. Aboriginal lawyer, Noel Pearson, says that 'native title [...] is all about what is left over. [...] And land rights have never been about the dispossession of the colonizers and their descendents. Whether it be statutory land rights or common law land rights—these land rights have always been focused on remnant lands.'[20] Sixteen per cent of the Australian continent is now owned or controlled by Aboriginal and Torres Strait Island people. And yet Graeme Neate, the President of the Native Title Tribunal, says:[21] 'It is my view that far too great a weight of expectation has been put on native title to deliver what it was not capable of delivering. There are areas of Australia where native title will deliver little or nothing.'

A country's system of land law and governance is undoubtedly more complex once indigenous land rights are recognized.

The cost of this complexity is high when a country like Australia has long delayed the recognition. The benefits to indigenous people are less and patchy when many of the dispossessed have had no option except to live away from their lands for generations. The complexity and patchiness provide no warrant for returning to the *terra nullius* mindset.

Formal Equality Under the Law, Land Rights, and Self-Determination

Equality does not mean treating everyone the same. If a law is to treat indigenous people differently from other citizens, indigenous people through their representatives should first give their consent and those indigenous citizens who want to receive the same treatment as other citizens should be able to opt out of the special arrangements for their own people and enjoy the usual benefits of citizenship. Sometimes the different treatment will be an undisputed added benefit to make up for past disadvantage or to accelerate access to the benefits of life in the postcolonial society. But there are instances when the treatment is adverse to individuals on the basis of their race or membership of a particular indigenous community. Their individual rights are to be foregone for the common good. The limits of self-determination for a community are now set when an individual claims not only the entitlements of community membership but also the human rights recognized in international instruments. The giving of young women in traditional marriage may be an integral part of traditional land holding arrangements but such practices must yield when a young woman wants the right to choose her husband. Traditional punishments such as spearing may assist elders to maintain public order, but the elders must surrender their authority when a young man insists on a trial in court and a punishment in jail.

If there still is a case for traditional marriage or traditional punishment, that case should be put by Aboriginal representatives who are attentive to the concerns of young Aboriginal women who want to choose their own husband and of young Aboriginal men who would prefer jail to spearing. Though these traditional practices may tie all community members to their land, kin, and ancestral meanings, they are practices which cannot be imposed on young persons living in two worlds, having watched more television episodes of *LA Law* and *Dallas* than I would ever want.

Forty years ago, there was controversy about the wage and employment conditions for Aborigines on vast pastoral properties in the north of Australia. Now the issue is access to social welfare payments and alcohol in Aboriginal communities. The denial of equal wages or personal social welfare payments or the denial of access to alcohol is a denial of formal equality under the law. Are there some social ramifications to the granting of formal equality that are so adverse to the common good of indigenous communities and the personal well-being of community members that the indigenous leaders in a self-determining community are not only entitled but also are right to forego the formal equality for their community members so that the community might advance its communal prospects?

In 1965, the Commonwealth Conciliation and Arbitration Commission was asked by the Australian Workers' Union to grant equal pay to Aborigines in the pastoral industry. These workers lived and worked on cattle and sheep properties in the remoter parts of Australia. The union called no evidence but simply enunciated the principle of equal pay.

The pastoralists called much evidence to demonstrate the problems and expected social effects of paying equal wages. Many Aborigines had lived on pastoral properties which were their traditional lands, receiving minimal pay for what the pastoralists regarded as minimal work. No Aborigines were called to give evidence about the effects. Sir James Gobbo, who was counsel for the Commonwealth government, revealed thirty years later that when he 'sought some such evidence I was instructed that there was no stockman suitable for the somewhat daunting task of giving evidence and being cross-examined'. Gobbo was deeply troubled but unable to do anything. He was receiving instructions from two government departments. The Department of Labour and Industry was adamant that all workers should be paid the same wage regardless of their race. The Department of Territories 'was very concerned about the impact of equal pay because of the risk to the existing arrangements on the stations. It would result in the abrupt end to the provision of steady employment and accommodation for Aborigines.'[22]

Sir John Kerr was counsel for the pastoralists. He submitted:[23] 'It seems to the pastoralists to be nonsense to say that men are better off, unemployed in thousands, but maintained in settlements in growing degrees of comfort when they could work in the real world with growing degrees of efficiency and growing economic reward.' The Commission acknowledged that massive disemployment was the likely result of granting equal wages. Once a stockman was unemployed, it was likely that he and his extended clan group would be moved off a pastoral lease which was on their traditional country. The effects of disemployment would be catastrophic for these small communities who had never known life in the economic mainstream. In its decision the Commission noted:[24]

> (If) aborigines are to be paid the same as whites, then employers would prefer to employ whites because they could employ far fewer with the same results. We accept the employers' evidence that as at present advised many of them expect to change over to white labour if aborigines are to be paid at award rates. We do not flinch from the results of this decision which we consider is the only proper one to be made at this point in Australia's history. There must be one industrial law, similarly applied to all Australians, aboriginal or not. If any problems of native welfare whether of employees or their dependants, arise as a result of this decision, the Commonwealth Government has made clear its intention to deal with them.

Employers were given twenty months' leeway to arrange for those Aborigines who were union members to be employed under award conditions. As predicted, many Aborigines were turned off pastoral properties, living in fringe camps on the outskirts of country towns and becoming long-term recipients of social welfare.

Government initiatives, including the purchase of pastoral properties for Aboriginal communities, the purchase of excisions on other pastoral properties, and preferential employment and education programs on remote Aboriginal communities have ameliorated some of the problems. But the payment of sit down money is now judged by government and many indigenous leaders to be no solution at all.

Andrew Robb, previously the Chief Executive of the National Farmers Federation and National Director of the Liberal Party, was recently elected to the Australian Parliament. In his maiden speech, he recalled his many visits to pastoral properties in Northern Australia after the granting of award wages and land rights. In his opinion, 'The land rights legislation was a totally inadequate response to the real issue—namely, the collapse of personal dignity and self-esteem among many Aboriginals, particularly the young.'[25] He compared the living circumstances of Aborigines on pastoral properties before and after land rights, before and after equal wages:

On many occasions, I would be taken to a bend in a river on a cattle station and shown where 100, 200 or 300 Aboriginals had lived for decades, with the men employed on the stations as stockmen and drovers, the older men as gardeners, and the women in the homestead. In many cases, schools were provided for the children. Aboriginal people were disadvantaged, but they had work and self-esteem, reasonable quality of life, strong mentoring from their elders, schooling and strict controls on alcohol.

Of course, all that ceased in the early 1970s following the understandable granting of equal wages in the pastoral industry, along with the misplaced provision of unfettered and generous welfare handouts. The related exodus of these people from their ancestral lands saw them living in settlements and on the fringes of towns. . . .

As I was driven around vast cattle stations, I witnessed cattlemen come across an Aboriginal elder known to them. The mutual respect was palpable. On the same day I saw the same cattlemen come across young Aboriginal men seriously affected by years of alcohol and aimlessness, young men stripped of any personal dignity or self-esteem. The cattlemen's contempt was palpable. The chilling fact is that the very fabric of a proud and fascinating culture, many thousands of years in the making, has been brought to its knees in less than 30 years by well-intentioned but seriously misguided policy.

For me the lesson is clear. People are very, very responsive to incentives, for good or bad. The wrong incentives, no matter how well meaning, can debilitate a community in no time. In this case, unconditional handouts have provided the seeds of destruction in a breathtakingly short period of time.

Forty years ago, no indigenous person participated in the decision or was even heard about the inevitable effects of granting equal wages. The members of one polity made decisions about those of the other polity without consulting them. Nowadays there is consultation. Those of us who are not indigenous are able to spare our consciences the moral quandary of choosing between conflicting goods—formal equality under the law, and government prescriptions which are race-based and race-targeted—by leaving the matter to discussion between government and indigenous leaders chosen and responsible through self-determining indigenous procedures.[26] But then we are troubled by the voice in the wilderness of other indigenous leaders who proclaim that their indigenous opponents have no option other than to do the government's bidding if they are to breathe the scarce political oxygen available for indigenous leaders in a society which has grown weary and doubtful about even medium term solutions for the plight of marginalized indigenous community members. It is even more troubling when government and/or the media decide which indigenous leaders will be given airplay regardless of their mode of selection as leaders or spokespersons. Indigenous leaders need credibility in both polities—the indigenous community and the mainstream society.

The Contemporary Problems of Indigenous Communities

In 1981, I was junior counsel in an Aboriginal murder trial in Queensland. Alwyn Peter was the fifteenth Aboriginal male in three years to have killed another Aboriginal person on an Aboriginal reserve. In these cases, the victim was usually the accused's woman partner. The senior defence counsel told the court that the homicide rate was the highest recorded among any ghetto group in the Western world. In each case, the accused and the victim were shaped by life on a reserve; and each in their own way was destroyed by it. To be a member of such a group, one did not have to be bad or mad; one had only to be Aboriginal. We defence lawyers had a good win in the *Peter* case. Having pleaded a defence of diminished responsibility, Alwyn walked free within weeks of the completion of the court proceedings. A woman anthropologist left me with the chilling observation that our forensic win had removed the one inadequate protection for defenceless women in remote Aboriginal communities—the minimal deterrence of the whitefella legal system. Meanwhile I was privileged to receive the last letter that the anthropologist W. E. H. Stanner ever wrote on 4 October 1981, he having been our key anthropological witness:

> I am fascinated by the question: how do general ideas about human conduct change so quickly? I can recall about fifty years ago appearing as a witness for the defence in an Aboriginal murder case in Darwin before Wells J. He was notably unimpressed by my arguments but nevertheless reluctantly took them into account in mitigation, while looking round the court as if expecting trouble. Or do I mean 'remarkably quickly'?

For the last twenty years, I have been preoccupied with the interrelatedness of Aboriginal dispossession, disadvantage, and marginalization and I have sought to articulate a publicly coherent policy of reconciliation, justice, and recognition for indigenous Australians. I do not come with the answers.

Recently, Noel Pearson, one of the most prominent Aboriginal spokesmen in Australia has opined that it was the 'symptom theory' that underpinned our approach to the *Alwyn Peter* case. Pearson says:[27]

All that was achieved by presenting a deeper historical understanding of the background to indigenous crimes and dysfunction was that the criminal justice system became sensitive to this background—and sentences became increasingly lenient. After a couple of decades we then reached a point where judges and observers—not the least Aboriginal people—started to wonder whether the loss of Aboriginal life was less serious than that of non-Aborigines. The criminal justice system may have tried to accommodate an understanding of the factors which Brennan and those who followed him had illuminated in the *Alwyn Peter* case, but it did nothing to abate offending and the resultant 'over representation' of indigenous people in the criminal justice system. In fact I would say that it made this problem worse.

These are troubling conclusions for any lawyer committed to justice according to law for all persons, including indigenous Australians who are more likely than any other group to be appearing in court for a custodial sentence. Once again, the proper application of law, including formal equality under the law, and the criminal law's attention to all relevant factors in the mitigation of punishment, may have unintended and negative consequences for the public order or common good of indigenous communities while displaying an admirable commitment to the human rights of the individual.

Life for the contemporary indigenous person is a life of choice and diverse possibilities. Law and social policy should provide the possibility of a realistic choice on a spectrum of possibilities from the pursuit of a traditional lifestyle on traditional lands to fully integrated participation in the social, economic, and political life of the nation state while maintaining cultural traditions and perspectives. In Australia, the resurgent opponents of land rights and self-determination think the former is not an option; thus this is an unreal choice, or at least a very cost ineffective choice. They argue for laws and policies which provide no option but accelerated access to the benefits of mainstream society or to the modern lifestyle which is not contingent on traditional cultural trappings.

Indigenous Australians may hold a secure title to 16 per cent of the land mass but their living conditions are still terrible. Twenty years ago, conservative politicians such as Sir Joh Bjelke Petersen were expressing concern that the granting or recognition of land rights would result in Aborigines being more removed from and less responsive to the health and education services of the mainstream community. At first, Sir Joh refused to discuss the possibility of land rights with the Commonwealth government.[28] He thought the Commonwealth's legislation in the Northern Territory in 1977 was 'carelessly introduced' and he was concerned that the granting of land rights and self management to Aboriginal communities in remote parts of Northern Australia could contribute to social isolation. In Queensland he was particularly critical of the Uniting Church which had encouraged Aborigines in their aspirations to return to traditional country setting-up outstations 'many miles from conventional facilities such as hospital, schools, etc, where reversion to the "tribal" pattern of life was encouraged':[29]

> School attendances dropped 40% and we cannot accept or tolerate a situation in this State where the young people of a community are thrust into an isolated situation, where by denial of fundamental

education and health care services, and by an ideological indoctrination of Aboriginal separation and separate development, they would, by contrast with all other Queenslanders, be seriously impaired in choosing to pursue broader horizons of life in the future should they wish to do so. That Aborigines may be socially and educationally equipped to make such a choice in life is the fundamental aim of our Aboriginal advancement policy.

These concerns are now being voiced by many indigenous leaders, not to decry land rights but to plead for government intervention aimed at improving the health, education, and employment prospects for Aborigines and Torres Strait Islanders living in their remote communities or seeking a life for their children in the urban areas of Australia. The children and grandchildren of Milirrpum, Mungurrawuy, Eddie Mabo, David Passi, and Alwyn Peter want to live in the best of all possible worlds, being Aboriginal but open to all the world has to offer, not being swamped by it, being able to stay afloat, able to make sense of it, able to embrace the mystery of it, even able to shape it, and to hand on to their children the uniqueness of their cultures and the universal possibilities of life in the modern world. Land rights secures the place for this to happen. The option of self-determination expands the possibilities within the limitations of the sovereign nation state. In Australia, life in the mainstream with some limited preferential access to a secured land base may turn out to be the preferred option for most Aborigines as well as for government. This will be an improvement on life in the mainstream with no secured land base addressing the historic dispossession. It will be different from living the life of a sovereign indigenous people, but with colonization that was never an option. It may also be very different from life on a self-determining community choosing the best of both lifestyles. This has appeal and possibility only for a minority of contemporary indigenous Australians. It must remain an option. Bridging the gap between life in two polities, under two laws, is the contemporary indigenous reality. It ought to be recognized and respected by the state.

The Challenges of the Future

Once a land base is secure, how do government and indigenous leaders find the balance between the individual rights of the indigenous community member and the collective entitlement of the community to order its affairs for the common good and cultural survival? Man does not live on bread alone. Man does not live on land alone. Aboriginal identity is tied to land, family, and the ancestral world of 'the Dreaming'. Unemployment, underemployment, alcohol and substance abuse are enormous problems in indigenous communities. Years ago I was riding in a four-wheel-drive truck in the Pitjantjara lands of South Australia after a big land rights meeting. On the back of the truck sat some Aboriginal youths huddled in blankets sniffing petrol. I wanted to stop the truck and do something. But what? One of the white community advisers told me that petrol sniffing was a legitimate expression of self-determination for a marginalized people without job prospects. These kids were addling their brains as we drove home. When parents do not take action, what role is there for indigenous leaders in co-operation with government to stop the truck and take action? Prime Minister Howard says:[30]

I think for the first time we are starting to see a recognition that the emphasis that's been placed on the rights and symbolic agenda over the last 20 or 30 years to the detriment of a greater sense of community responsibility and personal responsibility has been an error, and when you listen to the remarks of people like Noel Pearson and you hear their solutions in areas such as the Cape, you begin to understand that if communities are given a power to run their own affairs and to impose their own internal disciplines you will, over time, see an enormous improvement.

Howard thinks 'we ought to be listening a lot more to those who believe that self-responsibility and personal empowerment in Aboriginal communities and the end of the welfare mentality is essential before we bring about a profound change for the better.' But how is this to be done in the modern democratic state?

The Australian government and some of the more willing indigenous leaders have seized upon the idea of 'mutual obligation'. Under the first and most publicized mutual obligation agreement, the Mulan community in Western Australia agreed with government that parents and community leaders would attend to child hygiene and government would pay the cost of installing new petrol pumps. Aboriginal leader, Patrick Dodson, sees resonance between a conservative government's notion of mutual obligation and the traditional Aboriginal notion of reciprocity. But Dodson warns:[31] 'We don't want to see mutual obligation as a principle, or as a concept, trivialised by some of the stupidity that is associated with those contracts—like telling people to wash their kids' faces twice a day.'

Many advocates for indigenous rights bemoan the fact that indigenous leaders are not more united in their stand for land rights and self-determination. But a leader of an indigenous minority in a previously colonised society needs to act like an international statesman attentive to the domestic and international constituencies. In the politics of international relations, it has long been accepted that there are realists, liberals, and idealists. The realist is pessimistic about human nature and believes that the struggle for and exercise of power is central. The realist plays the government at their own game. The liberal 'contends that realism has a stunted vision that cannot account for progress', and the idealist 'illuminates the changing norms of sovereignty, human rights and international justice'. In Australia, an indigenous leader like Noel Pearson has a strong realist strand in his thinking, action, and advocacy. He deals with the government of the day. He uses their rhetoric and meets them on their ideological ground, seeking political leverage and real outcomes for his people. In 1993, he eye-balled Paul Keating on native title. Now he meets John Howard on mutual obligation. He says:[32]

> There is no argument with the principle of mutual obligation if we are going to get things fixed. The mistake we made in the past was to think indigenous salvation came from legal and political acts. This is part of it. But we must assume responsibility and recognise these things are achieved through social and economic progress.

With a more liberal strand, an indigenous leader like Pat Dodson will work within the limits set by government but insists that there is a broader agenda which is incomplete. Dodson says:[33]

> In Australia, the direction and emphasis of the reconciliation process and the position of Aboriginal people's unresolved issues with the nation are known points of difference between the Howard Government and Aboriginal people. We have agreed to work on what we have in common rather than what we may still disagree about, in search of a common good.

The Aboriginal people must come to terms with the Howard Government's social reform agenda in Aboriginal affairs. These are policies that stress mutual obligation and personal responsibility. . . .

This should never be interpreted as a rejection by the Aboriginal leadership in the struggle to have Aboriginal people in this country recognised as the first Australians and their rights to practise and enjoy their language, law and culture as the indigenous peoples of the nation. These are matters for future engagement and resolution, not matters to be discarded as irrelevant leftovers of another time and political reality.

Idealists demand that government play their game. An idealist like Michael Mansell insists that Aboriginal sovereignty is non-negotiable. Mansell says:[34]

Pearson's ideas are that any blame for Aboriginal disadvantage has more to do with Aboriginal recalcitrance than loss of land, or the extraordinary degree to which Aborigines have been dominated for so long.

The aim is to hurry up assimilation—push more Aboriginal kids into private schools, make people work or have the dole cut off, and participate within Australian society as a minority group.

A significant portion of the Aboriginal population believes the political foundation for an Aboriginal future is sovereignty. That base enables Aborigines to negotiate suitable political structures that promote Aboriginal identity, culturally sensitive education, a substantial land and economic base and political representation independent of white politicians.

This view has significant support within the Aboriginal population but little from white Australia.

As in international relations, the realist, liberal, and idealist perspectives all have their contribution to make 'providing the vocabulary and conceptual framework to ask hard questions of those who think changing the world is easy'.[35]

While Australia's indigenous leaders are seeking a way forward for their people in the short and long terms, the academic historians have been at war interpreting and re-interpreting the conflict and meeting between Aborigines and the colonizers. Following the publication of Keith Windschuttle's *The Fabrication of Aboriginal History*[36] Stuart McIntyre published *The History Wars*[37] and has now edited a collection entitled *The Historian's Conscience: Australian Historians on the Ethics of History.*[38] Greg Dening writes an essay in the latest collection entitled 'Living with and in deep time'. He recalls the celebration at the National Library in Canberra when two items of Australian heritage were placed on the Memory of the World Register. Those items, joining documents from other countries such as the Magna Carta and the US Declaration of Independence, were not the Australian Constitution or even the batting records of Donald Bradman, but rather Captain James Cook's journal from the Endeavour voyage of 1768–71 culminating in his hoisting the flag on Possession Island, and the papers relating to Eddie Mabo's case in the High Court. Dening describes the reverence with which he donned the cotton gloves to peruse these documents in the Manuscript Reading Room of the library. He takes up Eddie Mabo's drawings of his land and his people. This file 'needs a slow, slow read'. Dening says this file is Mabo's 'expression of how deep time has left its mark on the present'. Here is Dening's evocative description of his reading of these papers:[39]

He (Eddie Mabo) taps a truth the way we all tap truths from living, but in ways which need to be tolerated by those whose notion of law and evidence is blinkered by legal tradition and constitution and who need to find some entry into Eddie Mabo's otherness. The other papers in the Mabo Papers—of judges, lawyers, anthropologists, historians, witnesses of first people telling their stories—belong to the Memory of the World because the whole world faces the issue of how it lives with the Deep Time of all its first peoples, overrun and dispossessed as they are. It belongs to World Memory because the papers are we, the Australian people, struggling to do justice and to live with the Deep Time all around us. And we are in this instance the world.

Though land rights and self-determination provide no utopia for the contemporary indigenous Australian community, they have belatedly put right an ancient wrong. The cost and inconvenience are unavoidable. *Terra nullius* is no longer an option. The Australian novelist Tim Winton reminds us, 'The past is in us, and not behind us. Things are never over.'[40] The words of Chief Justice Marshall in *Johnson* v *McIntosh* still ring out today:[41]

> [H]umanity demands, and a wise policy requires, that the rights of the conquered to property should remain unimpaired; that the new subjects should be governed as equitably as the old, and that confidence in their security should gradually banish the painful sense of being separated from their ancient connections, and united by force to strangers.

We Australians belatedly have come to the right starting point on an endless search for justice between indigenous and non-indigenous citizens. Though it is no longer fashionable or politically correct in Australia, there is no getting away from Prime Minister Keating's insight that we white Australians must start with an act of recognition:[42]

> Recognition that it was we who did the dispossessing. We took the traditional lands and smashed the traditional way of life. We brought the disasters. The alcohol. We committed the murders. We took the children from their mothers. We practised discrimination and exclusion.

> It was our ignorance and our prejudice. And our failure to imagine these things being done to us. With some noble exceptions, we failed to make the most basic human response and enter into their hearts and minds. We failed to ask—how would I feel if this were done to me?
>
> As a consequence, we failed to see that what we were doing degraded all of us.

These sentiments should rightly continue to haunt all citizens of post-colonial societies where indigenous people 'united by force to strangers', still live on the fringes. With a confident identity and secure sense of belonging in both worlds, indigenous people might 'gradually banish the painful sense of being separated from their ancient connections'. Those citizens who are recent migrants are joined with the descendants of the colonizers, accepting the national responsibility of correcting past wrongs so that the descendants of the land's traditional owners might belong to their land, their kin, and their Dreaming in the society built upon their dispossession. While we continue to blame the victims, we are haunted by Andrew Robb's observation from the opposite side of the parliamentary chamber echoing the Keating declaration. In his maiden speech to the Australian parliament, Robb said, 'We have basically poisoned recent generations; poisoned their bodies with alcohol and other substances and poisoned their spirit and self-belief with handouts and welfare dependency.'[43] Land rights and self-determination are necessary but insufficient antidotes for indigenous minorities wanting to belong in post-colonial societies coming to terms with their history. Just because the indigenous people amongst us also need work and education, that is no reason to deny them their land rights and self-determination.

Response to Frank Brennan, Standing in Deep Time; Standing in the Law: A Non-indigenous Australian Perspective on Land Rights, Land Wrongs, and Self-Determination

Marcus Colchester

In his thought-provoking presentation, Frank Brennan speaks as an Irish-Australian, who has campaigned for, and critiqued, Aboriginal rights for most of his life. Framing his arguments within, and beyond, the confines of British Commonwealth jurisprudence, he insists that historical injustices and the consequent demoralization of indigenous peoples must be addressed by recognizing indigenous peoples' collective rights to their lands and to self-determination. Yet, while firm and convincing in his position, he also cautions us against too blinkered an approach. Collective rights, he argues, should not be asserted at the expense of individual rights and freedoms. Nor will the recognition of rights, alone, be enough to recover the morale of oppressed indigenous peoples suffering the collapse of personal dignity and self-esteem that has stemmed from centuries of discrimination and social exclusion.[1]

His insights are especially relevant to those of us in Britain who share his concern for human rights and the plight of indigenous peoples. Shockingly, our current government not only denies that there are collective human rights but is actively blocking agreement at the United Nations of the draft Declaration on the Rights of indigenous Peoples. The government justifies its objections, at least in part, by arguing that assertion of collective rights imperils individual rights.

The draft Declaration is a document that grew out of ten years of standard setting work at the Working Group on indigenous Populations of the UN's Sub-Commission on Human Rights.[2] Drawing on the testimony and experience of indigenous peoples and governments alike, the Working Group assembled a unique body of information about the situation of indigenous peoples and the measures that will most effectively provide remedy for the abuses that they continue to suffer. The legal and political gains already made by indigenous peoples in Australia, New Zealand, Canada, USA, and Scandinavia were critical to this process, as were the testimonies of indigenous peoples from developing countries.

The Working Group recorded in painful detail the experiences of indigenous peoples from all corners of the globe exposed to: genocide; gross human rights violations; the arbitrary expropriation of indigenous peoples' territories and natural resources and their forced resettlement to make way for mines, oil and gas development, dams, agribusiness, logging, plantations, colonization schemes, and conservation; denial of the value of their cultures and religions, even the right to speak their own languages; limitations on their citizenship, rights of domicile, to vote and participate in national political processes; the denial of their right to govern themselves in line with their own traditions and customary laws and to represent themselves through their own representative institutions.

Taking into account this reality and the long-term consequences of this denial of rights, manifest in the kinds of self-abuse and loss of identity and self-esteem that Brennan calls to our attention, the Declaration calls on states to recognize the too long denied rights of indigenous peoples.

The Declaration is founded on two key principles of international human rights law. In the first place, the Declaration affirms the principle of equality and non-discrimination, that indigenous peoples enjoy the same rights and freedom as others. In the second place, it draws on the fundamental principle of the United Nations Charter, also affirmed in the United Nations Covenants on Civil and Political Rights and Economic Social and Cultural Rights, that all peoples have the right to self-determination. Accordingly, Article 3 of the Declaration asserts: 'indigenous peoples have the right of self-determination. By virtue of that right they freely determine their political status and freely pursue their economic, social and cultural development.' The rest of the Declaration then flows from these two propositions.[3] The Declaration thus affirms the collective rights of indigenous peoples to live in freedom, peace, and security, to be protected against genocide, to maintain their distinct identities as peoples, not to be subjected to imposed policies of assimilation, and not to be forcibly removed from their lands (Articles 6–11). It likewise proclaims their rights to their cultural, religious, spiritual and linguistic identities and cultural heritage (Articles 12–14), and affirms their rights to appropriate control over their education and protection of their labour (Articles 15–18). The Declaration anticipates that indigenous peoples will form parts of wider national polities and thus affirms their rights to participation, development, and other economic and social rights (Articles 19–25).

At the core of the Declaration are Articles 26–30, setting out indigenous peoples' collective rights to own, develop, and control their lands, territories, and natural resources, to restitution of lands that have been taken from them, to their cultural and intellectual properties and to the right to free, prior, and informed consent to any projects proposed on their lands. The right, in other words, to say 'No' to outsiders' impositions, not as individuals but as self-organized groups. Their right to self-determination implies the right to self-government and appropriate forms of autonomy, to determine their citizenship in accordance with custom, to maintain their own juridical systems and have the treaties they have entered into recognized and enforced (Articles 31–6).

During the nearly two decades of debate at the United Nations that these standards were elaborated, debated, and consolidated, the representatives of Her Majesty's Government of the United Kingdom remained largely silent. They likewise acquiesced when the International Labour Congress adopted in 1989 ILO Convention No. 169 on indigenous and Tribal Peoples in Independent Countries, a document replete with collective rights. They did not demur when, in 1993, the draft Declaration elaborated by the Working Group was adopted by the Sub-Commission. They nodded through the decision, in 1994, of the Human Rights Commission to establish an Open Ended Working Group, tasked with discussing and, if possible, agreeing the text of the Declaration. They did not object when the United Nations General Assembly agreed, in 1994, to an International Decade on the World's indigenous People, one of the objectives of which was indeed to finalize and adopt the Declaration. Their voices were hardly heard during the first five years of deliberations at the Open Ended Working Group, when the text of the

Declaration began to be analysed first in terms of general principles and then phrase by phrase.

Only in the last three years has the British Government taken it into its collective head to question, and indeed place on record formal objections to, the key provisions of the Declaration. Astonished by this behaviour a number of British human rights groups have asked the Government for an explanation, leading to two rather unproductive meetings between the Foreign and Commonwealth Office and NGOs and indigenous representatives.

According to the Human Rights Policy Department of the Foreign and Commonwealth Office:

> The UK has a clear position on the idea of collective human rights: with the exception of the right of self-determination (ICCPR Article 1.1) we do not accept the concept of collective human rights. In a legal framework, human rights are calls upon states to treat individuals in accordance with international standards. As a result, the UK is unwilling to accept use of the term *rights of indigenous peoples* in a human rights context.[4]

In the follow-up meeting the FCO has argued that human rights are a product of negotiated agreements between nation states at the United Nations, are limited to those agreements and are essentially rights of individuals with respect to these states.

In adopting such an isolated view of human rights, the British Government sets aside a number of pieces of international law that recognize collective human rights, denies the relevance of the jurisprudence of the UN human rights committees, which regularly censure governments for failing to respect the collective rights of indigenous peoples, and ignores the historical relations that Britain has had with indigenous peoples in many parts of the world.[5] This is troubling enough, but it also flies in the face of the demands of indigenous peoples themselves. Whereas indigenous peoples argue, like Brennan, that recognition of their collective rights is essential to redress the historical injustices they have suffered, the UK government argues that these ills can be as well addressed through respect for their individual rights.

However, the provisions of the Declaration are exactly the kinds of rights that cannot be reduced to individual rights. Self-determination is a collective right and forms of self-government, autonomy, the exercise of customary law, and negotiation of treaties are all likewise the rights of collectives not of individuals. The parcelling-up of collectively owned and managed lands into individual holdings has been one of the main processes of dispossession of indigenous peoples.[6] The need for indigenous peoples to have the right to collective representation and to free, prior, and informed consent and negotiated agreements with incoming mines, dams, logging, and conservation schemes has been recognized and accepted by a whole series of international policy reviews.[7] A very large number of countries, especially in the Americas, have recognized these collective rights in their Constitutions and other laws, while the collective rights of peoples are strongly asserted in the African Charter of Peoples and Human Rights.[8] Those who know indigenous peoples' situations best, in other words, are clear that collective rights are crucial to righting the wrongs they suffer.

Indigenous peoples have been demanding justice by invoking international human rights standards at the United Nations for nearly thirty years. In doing so, they have not been blind to the importance of themselves adhering to these same standards and ensuring that their collective right to self-determination does not lead to indifference to, or lead to violations of, the individual rights of indigenous persons. The issue has most strongly come to the fore in discussions about the rights of indigenous women.[9] In the 2000 'Manila Declaration', indigenous peoples accepted that the concept of justice is universal and that in

> revalidating the traditions and institutions of our ancestors, it is also necessary that we ourselves honestly deal with those ancient practices, which may have led to the oppression of indigenous women and children. However, the conference also stresses that the transformation of indigenous systems must be defined and controlled by indigenous peoples . . . [as] part of the right to self-determination.[10]

In practice, many indigenous peoples who have secured a measure of self-governance and the effective exercise of customary law, accept the right of indigenous persons to have recourse to national courts and international tribunals when they feel their individual rights are not being upheld.[11]

Contrary to the assertions of the British Government, the draft Declaration on the Rights of indigenous Peoples does not risk diminishing individual rights. Article 33 expressly notes that 'indigenous peoples have the right to promote, develop and maintain their institutional structures and their distinctive juridical customs, traditions, procedures and practices, in accordance with internationally recognized human right standards', while Article 45 expressly affirms that 'Nothing in this Declaration may be interpreted as implying for any State, group or person any right to engage in any activity or to perform any act contrary to the Charter of the United Nations.'

4

If this is your Land, where are your Stories?

Ken Wiwa

Land rights are a contentious issue anywhere in the world, but perhaps nowhere are they more controversial than in Africa, where land has lasting historical—and deep spiritual—significance. Perhaps until the continent is able to reconcile itself to the land question it will never resolve its social, political, and economic dysfunctions. I myself have spent the last ten years of my life trying to resolve the complexities of a story that revolves around the issue of land rights. I am referring of course to my involvement in my community's struggle for social justice in Nigeria. That question will occupy the bulk of the personal reflection that follows, though it will also leave room for some more general observations on the impact and consequences of the struggle for land rights in Africa.

Before I begin, however, it may be necessary to issue a caveat. (When you're speaking about an issue as emotive as land rights, there can never be enough caveats.) Most importantly, I want to insist that I have come to offer my thoughts on the matter from the perspective of a storyteller. In case this sounds unseasonably portentous, I should probably explain myself. There is a tradition of storytellers in my Ogoni community. They are known as *wiayor.* A *wiayor* is often an ordinary member of the community who is picked out by our ancestors and blessed with a prophetic vision of the future. Often the *wiayor* bears a message that the community may not be disposed to hear: he has frequently been sent to deliver a story warning the community that it must abandon its traditions. Nevertheless, the *wiayor* has no choice but to go back to his community and convey that message to the people. If he ducks this duty he will be cursed and condemned by the ancestors; if he takes up the challenge he also faces the wrath of the community for bringing bad news. One might say that in Ogoni culture the *wiayor* tradition approximates to the myth of Cassandra.

The *wiayor* is the muse of the Ogoni storyteller and it was in that noble but troubling tradition that my father, Ken Saro-Wiwa, saw himself as following. As you can imagine, it is not a tradition that anyone seeks out. It finds you. Indeed, this bitter-sweet gift is usually visited on the shy, retiring type: an authentic *wiayor* would never attempt, or at least would usually be unwilling, to arrogate such authority to himself. For my own part, I should confess that I never knew we had such traditions in my community until I spent two years writing my last book, *In the Shadow of a Saint*, which began its shelf life as a self-serving attempt to explain why I was unwilling to take up the struggle that my father had lived and died for. It was while I was trying to write myself a loophole in my contract with my community that I came across one of Ken Saro-Wiwa's unpublished essays, in which he explains his literary calling in terms of the *wiayor* tradition. Now I am loath to say what effect that discovery has had on me. Rather, I offer this long preamble by way of issuing my caveat that I am here to talk about land rights as a story.

Those of you who appreciate the full value of stories know that we are nothing if not the sum of our stories; our maps, our laws, our history, our culture, and even our buildings and tombstones. All these are but different ways of telling stories. As J. Edward Chamberlain (from whom, I confess, I stole the title of this lecture) wrote:

> Stories have given shape and meaning to our sense of ourselves as individuals, cultures and nations, we are both connected by these stories and separated by their different truths. Whether Jew or Arab, black or white, Muslim or Christian, Catholic or Protestant, man or woman, our stories hold us in thrall and others at bay.

The title of this talk, and indeed the title of Edward Chamberlain's excellent book, is taken from an encounter between an Indian community in north-west British Columbia and some government officials. The officials had come to claim the land for the government and the natives were amazed by the claim. It was one of the elders who raised the question: if this is your land then where are your stories? That question goes right to the heart of the matter of land rights in Africa. For another way of asking the question for Africa is what kind of stories are being told about Africa? Who is telling the story and is it the right story? Does the story do justice to the people who have lived on and from the land for generations and does the story uphold their rights?

There is certainly no shortage of Western stories about Africa, many of them peddled in the Western news media. Perhaps the prevailing narrative is that of Africa as an overcrowded, poor continent. But there is another side to that story. Africa is not a poor continent. Africa is rich: rich in human and social capital, rich in its diverse cultures and in its own knowledge systems, and rich—of course—in land and mineral resources. India is more populous than Africa yet you can fit the land mass of India, China, Europe, America, Argentina, and New Zealand into Africa and still have room to spare. Africa is much bigger than most of us could reckon with yet it has been diminished, reduced to scale on our mental maps and listed as a liability in the global inventory.

At the present time it is near impossible to open a newspaper without reading about the problems facing Africa, or an editorial on the latest 'fix-Africa' plan. The cynic might be tempted to dismiss all this noise as yet another example of how Africa is being cast as backdrop for those who need to display their social conscience on their political sleeves. A more generous reading of such stories might argue that no matter what shape or disguise it comes in, Africa needs all the help it can get: an old African saying advises that 'if the devil gives you a scholarship, grab it with both hands'. Whichever view we take, however, current discourse on Africa, however well-meaning, is depressingly familiar. Take the World Economic Forum, which I recently attended. There I heard much of the usual talk of the villains that plague Africa: poverty, corruption, lack of good governance. But while the customary carrot and stick was very much in evidence—how *will* we get these recalcitrant Africans to mend their dirty ways?—there was precious little in the way of a full reckoning, or even a token acknowledgement that there are at least two sides to every story. (As can never be repeated quite often enough, the other side of the corruption story is of course that for a bribe to be accepted it has to have been offered.)

If we truly want to tackle poverty in Africa, then the rich West must take a hard and unflinching look at its role in that story. Many of us in Africa know the individuals and corporations who made their fortunes and built their empires and cities on the back of the slave trade. We know those who profited under apartheid, those who collaborated with murderers and despots in the name of a Cold War that was a hot war for the millions who died at the hands of a Mobutu or Idi Amin. We know the people who hoard public funds that have been stolen from the public purse or those who feed off enormous kickbacks for corrupt government officials. We know the people who sell arms, rape the environment and destroy the fragile ecosystems of the continent. We know that these people and their organizations have been allowed to get away with the theft of Africa's natural resources. In less polite and accommodating company they would also have been charged with racketeering and sued for exploitation, as accomplices to mass murder and genocide. For if the truth be told the profits and assets that were built in Africa have been transferred from the continent, laundered and institutionalized, and now lie hidden behind layers of respectability, brand name, and well out of reach of domestic and international law.

It seems clear to me that as long as Africa is being described as an irredeemable basket case then the prescriptions for its recovery will only ever address what are the symptoms and not the root causes of Africa's dysfunction. I say this knowing full well that there is poverty in Africa. After all, you do not have to look far to find it. But, as someone once told me, an African does not wake up in the morning and wonder 'how am I going to reduce my poverty today?' Rather, the root of the problem—and yes, if you like, the blame—for the impoverishment of Africa's inventory are complex matters. I see that root as fixed deep in the story of the land.

If I were a poet I'd suggest that the only way to tackle the root and branch of Africa's dysfunctions is to tear up the map of the continent and redraw it, then painstakingly replot its political and cultural boundaries from the 800 million individual stories on the continent. But since poets build castles in the air and soldiers do the marching on the ground, then pragmatism must rule. Nonetheless—and I will return to this idea—no fix-Africa plan is ever going to work unless there is a determination that all those who have profited from misery are held to account. Of course, no sooner do such proposals hit the table, than all kinds of lawyers, accountants, and investors will give you a million and one reasons why it is impractical and even suicidal. I would reluctantly have to agree. But these difficulties themselves only exist because African politics is back to front: the very people who should be insisting on redrawing the map of Africa would actually be doing themselves out of a job.

This back-to-frontness can be a frustrating business. For example, one of the great frustrations of the old OAU, which now appears to have been adopted as a guiding principle of the African Union, is the principle of non-interference in the domestic affairs of other nations. When it comes to land reform and restitution for past injustice, this principle dictates that it must always be an internal matter, conducted within the constraints and boundaries of nations that only exist because someone else imposed their story on the indigenous people. These borders remain the greatest and seemingly intractable obstacle to real and fundamental change in Africa. For as long as that history continues to underwrite the present then the long-term obstacle to social justice in Africa will be shaped by a set of rules that tends to favour property rights over human rights.

This tension between property rights and human rights seems to me fundamental. In the simplest and most essentializing form of the distinction, the colonizer/settler tends to favour property rights while the colonized/indigenous bases their claim on a spiritual attachment to the land. Whether this spiritual attachment can be translated unproblematically into the Western language of rights is of course a difficult matter, and one which risks leading off into the kind of theoretical territory which, while doubtless of crucial importance, would prove distracting here. For the sake of convenience, I shall continue to refer to claims based on spiritual attachments to land as claims for 'rights' which, whatever the difficulty in theory, certainly retain a basis in indigenous experience. I hope that you will view any resultant gaps, contradictions, or begged questions as nourishing others' discussion of these problems, rather than disabling my own.

Nowhere is the conflict between property rights and land rights so clearly expressed as in southern Africa—a region whose recent experiences make for an interesting comparison with my own in Nigeria. Zimbabwe constitutes perhaps the most extreme example; for reasons of time, and of my relative lack of expertise in the affairs of that country, I shall focus on South Africa.

In South Africa land reform has had to negotiate and navigate this tension between the pragmatism of property rights against the moral, historical, emotional, and spiritual force of the people's right to the land. The history of land in South Africa followed the familiar narrative that is common all over Africa—one of dispossession and displacement. According to an old African cliché, before the white man came to Africa we had the land and they had the Bible. Then they said 'let us pray', and when we opened our eyes we had the Bible and they had the land. Once land had been appropriated and stolen from Africans, all too often in the name of God, Apartheid governments passed laws for the express purpose of removing non-whites from prime property and closer to agricultural employment. The new property to which most blacks were relocated was not registered. The implementation of racially based land laws resulted in 87 per cent of the total land area ending up in the hands of the white minority. Meanwhile 13 per cent was 'set aside' for the 5 to 1 black majority.

This situation was clearly untenable in a country once majority rule was restored. The end of Apartheid was rightly seen by the masses as their opportunity to redress 500 years of injustice. But it has not been easy to balance the sacred weight of history against the pragmatic needs of today. Mindful of capital flight and the impact on the economy, not to mention peace and political stability, the government's land reform has been relatively slow. The lack of title deeds in former homelands, the lack of training and start-up capital on redistributed farms and a restitution programme which, in practice, favours financial compensation over actual land restoration by as much as 3:1 has slowed down reform. The Land Claims Court has delivered only 331 judgments by 20 December 2004 and land invasions are on the increase. When I was last in South Africa late last year, I heard people voice fears that the land issue in South Africa is potentially more problematic and explosive than the situation in Zimbabwe.

Since the end of Apartheid the land redistribution programme has transferred only 1.4 million hectares from white to black owners. Meanwhile, the land restitution programme has transferred just 512,912 hectares of land in the resolution of more than half of the 68,878 claims lodged. Together, these total land transfers through land reform represent less than 2.3 per cent of South Africa's estimated 85 million hectares of agricultural land, and even less of the country's total 122 million hectares land mass. Land reform transfers have benefited barely 250,000 households, or just over a million people. As a result, South Africa continues to have 19 million poor and landless rural people and 7 million poor and landless urban people. Taken together, these constituencies represent about 60 per cent of the population. Department of Land Affairs statistics suggest that the majority of restitution claims settled so far have been resolved through financial compensation, a mechanism that does not result in any land reform taking place.

I have to confess that my investigation into the land issue in South Africa informed and impressed on me that land reform is not a simple case of acquiring and distributing the land. In a paper entitled 'The End of Restitution', Andries Du Toit suggests that rural development initiatives are all too often undermined by sentimental conceptions that underestimate the levels of fragmentation and division that pertains in many rural (and urban) settlements, the diversity of interests and agendas that emanate from within them, and the exploitation and manipulative relationships that exist between communities. The situation is further aggravated by the reality that there are people who sacrificed their lives fighting for the right to regain their land, only to find themselves subjected to seemingly impenetrable bureaucratic processes. The requirement to submit affidavits, marriage certificates, and many other documents disillusions potential claimants and obscures the process. According to a former Regional Land Claim Commissioner for the Western and Northern Cape, 'all claimants must recognise that lodging a claim is not like claiming a bag of potatoes'. Claims must be submitted to the Commission of the Restitution of Land Rights, whose task is to investigate the merits of claims and then to settle them through mediation.

Andries du Toit asks: can South Africa afford restitution? In his attempts to answer the question he argues:

> the reality is that South Africa does not have these resources in plentiful supply. South Africa is a poor country . . . demands on it are many and likely to increase and the land claimants are not the only deserving cause that we can find . . . But the reality is that there are many other victims who morally and politically can and will make equally strong claims: from the victims of Bantu Education . . . to those discriminated against by the unequal provision of basic health care in apartheid South Africa.

In short, and to conclude these brief reflections on South Africa, you can see that even in a newly minted state, where majority rule by a party broadly elected on a mandate to redress the injustices of the past, land reform in such a context faces difficult choices in its path to social justice. Between the moral imperatives of land rights and the pragmatism of property rights there is no easy walk to freedom.

Before turning, by way of comparison, to the Ogoni experience, I should like to draw your attention to the conclusions of a conference held in London in November 2004, entitled 'Land in Africa: market asset or secure livelihood?' The conference was a gathering of African ministers, policy makers, opinion leaders, and researchers concerned with land issues who came together with representatives from international agencies and experts on land in Africa to 'explore current thinking and experience with land tenure issues across the continent'. Out of the debates on how land policies and programmes for land management can best promote secure rights, investment, and economic growth, a number of policy messages emerged. Since the conference may shape the parameters of the land issue, I should like to provide, in passing, a brief summary of its conclusions.

Land in Africa: Market Asset or Secure Livelihood?

Secure land rights are now recognized by most African governments as critical for peace, stability, and economic growth. The African Union also sees better governance of land and natural resources as central to all hopes of peace and stability across the continent. There are increasing demands for land and there are tensions stemming from competition for this valuable resource. African governments must take the lead in land policy and tenure reform, since political interests are at stake. A diverse array of approaches to strengthening land rights is now emerging, from which stem valuable lessons to be shared between governments, civil society groups, and land professionals. Important questions concern how pan-African and South-South exchanges can strengthen such a learning approach; and what the G8 can best do to support an African-led agenda on land.

1. Equitable Access to Land Lies at the Heart of Democracy and Sustainable Development
    - Secure land rights are critical to economic growth, and to equipping African agriculture to face the challenges of a globalizing world.
    - The history of land settlement, conquest, and market development in Africa needs to be grasped to understand the current context, and find ways forward.
    - Secure rights are important for all so that the millions of small farmers who depend on agriculture for their livelihoods can survive and prosper, alongside larger investors.

- At the same time the growth and importance of Africa's cities poses a major challenge for urban and peri-urban land management.
- Government ownership, use, and management of land needs to become more accountable.
- Public dialogue needs to be strengthened and supported by the development of civil society actors and knowledge networks both of which have important roles to play.
- Land is also relevant to the peace and security agenda.
- Competition for land and natural resources plays a major role in generating wider conflict and insecurity. Establishing an accountable basis for managing land is an important element of institution-building in post conflict settings.

2. Innovation and Change in Land Rights Management Illustrate Diverse Ways of Delivering Secure Rights to Africa's Land and Natural Resource Users

- A diverse range of relatively simple, low cost, accessible approaches using local institutions and modern technology have been developed in different parts of Africa, which aim to secure rights for all.
- Care is needed in formalizing property rights through individual land title to ensure that poor people's rights to use and access land and resources are protected.
- Women's rights are particularly vulnerable; in addition to equitable policies and laws, practical measures to promote gender inclusion at all levels are needed. The rising incidence of HIV/AIDS makes women even more vulnerable to dispossession.

- Conserving Africa's common property resources is vital for a wide range of natural resources users. Maintaining access to the commons is especially important for the livelihoods of poor people. Strengthening group resource management, legal recognition of joint ownership, and developing management agreements between different users provide essential ingredients for securing the commons.

3. The G8 Together with the African Union and Member states can Help Build Sound Policies and Institutions to Secure Land Rights for all.

   - The UK's chairmanship of the G8 in 2005 offers a unique opportunity to secure the place of land issues in the long term partnership between Africa and the world's richest nations. Although specific commitments of resources may be needed in the short term, the last five years have demonstrated that gradual but solid progress can be made in developing appropriate policies and practical approaches. What is needed now is a sustained commitment to collaboration from the G8.

Now I've suggested earlier that I would prefer to suspend judgement on the latest fix-Africa initiative until I am convinced that it will actually deliver on its promises or at least succeed where previous fix-Africa programmes have failed. One of the reasons why I am somewhat sceptical is that in thinking about my own community's issues around land rights it seems clear to me that there needs to be more of a bottom-up rather than top-down approach to land issues in Africa.

I think it is important to acknowledge, as I suggested earlier, that the only way to build a mutually reinforcing consensus on land rights is to renegotiate the terms and conditions by which African communities engage with national or even global economic and political systems. Unless we reconfigure the system on a sustainable and equitable basis then the choice will be more window dressing of the status quo or, as in the case of South Africa, a drawn-out compromise.

As things stand my community is at an interesting point of departure on that journey. So let me explain.

I am an Ogoni. That means I am one of an estimated 500,000 people who live on 404 square miles of an oil-rich and fertile plateau of the Niger River Delta in southern Nigeria. We have lived in this place for anything from 400 years to since time began, depending on which of our histories, oral or written, you subscribe to. The Ogoni (my father used to encourage us to say Ogoni rather than Ogoniland or the Ogoni people, to emphasize the symbiotic relationship between land and people) were never involved in the slave trade. We were largely an isolated community until the British arrived on the scene in the late nineteenth/early twentieth century. Our eventual absorption into the British protectorate of Southern Nigeria was effected without consultation but by a decision made at the treaty of Berlin in 1884. The terms of the treaty, signed literally and figuratively in another world, gave Queen Victoria the right to exploit the geographical space now known as Nigeria.

During the nineteenth century the Niger Delta was a lucrative sphere of commerce for the British, especially its palm oil merchants. But it was the discovery of another kind of oil—crude oil—in 1956 that really changed the dynamics of the relationship between the world and the indigenous peoples of the Niger River Delta. Oil was discovered in Nigeria in 1956 and in Ogoni two years later. Since 1958 an estimated 900 million barrels of oil have been pumped out of my community. But instead of benefiting from this resource, the presence of oil companies has proved to be a curse for the people and the land. A region that ought to be as rich as a small gulf state remains grossly underdeveloped. Pipe-borne water is still non-existent, the electricity supply is barely functional, schools and health services are perennially underfunded, churning out graduates that are barely educated in the skills to make informed decisions in a hi-tech world of the knowledge economy. This pathetic distribution of social services is what we have to show for the estimated 30billion of oil that we have contributed to Nigeria's bank account. To compound my community's misery, the activities of an unregulated, largely unaccountable oil industry have compromised our existence. The oil industry made enormous profits from Ogoni largely because it was not pressed to pay attention to the impact of their operations on the social, economic, ecological, and cultural fortunes of its host community.

In 1990 my people took stock of the situation and concluded that we were getting a raw deal both from the Nigerian government and the oil industry. It was then that my father, Ken Saro-Wiwa, formed MOSOP (the Movement for the Survival of the Ogoni People). In his vision of what was a non-violent grassroots organization, my father hoped that MOSOP would not only sensitize our people to what was happening to the land, the people, and our culture, but that MOSOP would also mobilize the community to stand up for our rights. So successful was MOSOP's mobilization of the community that on 4 January 1993, an estimated 300,000 Ogoni came out in support of the aims and ideals of MOSOP during a peaceful protest march. Shell was declared *persona non grata* and served a quit notice to stay away from Ogoni until the company paid back rents and cleaned up its operations. In response, Shell pulled out of Ogoni claiming that some of its workers had been attacked.

Instead of arbitrating between the demands of the community and the concerns of the oil companies, the military government of Nigeria responded by trying to intimidate the community into silence. The dictatorship's response was predictable. Oil accounts for 90 per cent of Nigeria's foreign exchange revenues and the billions of dollars that accrue from oil is what attracts soldiers to politics in Nigeria. So although Ogoni only accounts for a small proportion of the oil from the Niger Delta, the military government viewed the implications of a small community driving a multinational from its land as a threat to national security. With this in mind, Nigeria's then military dictator General Abacha sent in soldiers to—and I quote—'Rid Ogoni of the MOSOP virus . . . to enable oil production to resume'.

After the Ogoni leaders and people had spoken with one voice in January 1993, our leaders and people experienced rising levels of harassment and intimidation. The commitment of some was bought off, sowing a climate of confusion and mutual suspicion within the community. This served, as it had been calculated to serve, to undermine the collective purpose of a community that had been united under MOSOP. Following the brutal murder of four Ogoni chiefs during a riot in Ogoni on 21 May 1994, my father and scores of other MOSOP activists were arrested and held in connection with the murders of the four chiefs, whom the government described as moderate and pro-government. The next day the military administrator of the region held a press conference where he paraded a bag of bones alleged to be the remains of the murdered chiefs. Lt Colonel Dauda Komo declared that he was satisfied that the investigations were complete and singled out what he described as MOSOP thugs and radicals to fit the crime.

My father and the other so-called 'suspects' were held for nine months without trial. When they were finally charged they were brought before a military tribunal, the very same military that had openly declared war on the Ogoni. My father was accused of inciting his supporters to murder the four chiefs. After nine months of a trial that was roundly condemned by jurists and international observers, the presiding judge sentenced my father and eight other defendants to death. Ten days later they were hanged.

This story is now well known, notorious. But it is important that it be told and retold for several reasons. Not least among these is the fact that although we now have a civilian government in place in Nigeria, indeed a government that was largely elected in the wake of the international outcry and fall-out from the execution of the Ogoni nine, that government's record in the Niger Delta, much less in Ogoni, is unimpressive. Having made token efforts at a truth and reconciliation process, the government did not take long to move on to its real agenda, namely to try to persuade the rest of the world that Nigeria was now safe for business and foreign investment. Meanwhile, and predictably, Shell has splashed public relations money to greenwash its hands of its responsibilities and role in the Ogoni tragedy and the Niger Delta. All of which adds up to this: ten years after the world's attention was drawn to the situation in the Niger Delta, and six years into a supposedly democratic administration, the social, political, and economic problems of the Niger Delta have, if anything, escalated. You are all aware of the increasing levels of violence in the region as a whole. In Ogoni, at least, there has been an uneasy peace since my father and others were executed. Shell has not returned to Ogoni and has increasingly come to understand that such is the depth of resentment in the community that it cannot hope to return.

Amid this uneasy peace, Ogoni stands, as I said before, at a crucial moment in its history. For the Nigerian government is pushing for a resumption of what it cryptically calls 'economic activity', and there are voices in the community who feel the time is right to consider that option. My own view is that we always welcome the resumption of economic activity in Ogoni as long as it is consistent with the aims and ideals enshrined in the Ogoni Bill of Rights. The Bill of Rights was adopted by universal acclaim of my people in 1990. Circumstances might have dated some of the details of the document but the fundamentals remain: which it is intolerable that a community has provided so much of its natural resources to a company and a country should have received so little in return.

The greatest obstacle to progress in Ogoni remains the arrogance and cowardice of Shell. That a corporation which recently posted the largest profits in its history refuses to account for its human rights and environmental abuses is a moral stain on its conscience. For years now we have been trying to hold the Nigerian government and bring Shell Oil to account for their actions in Ogoni. We have succeeded in bringing a case against Shell in the district courts of New York and the case has already reached pre-trial. However, Shell is using its considerable legal resources to delay its day in court: this year we hope the world will ask Shell, which has admitted it has made mistakes, to stand up and be accountable for those mistakes.

The more I have thought about the Ogoni struggle over the last five years the more it has impressed me that my community has actually been presented with an opportunity to transform its society. For the issue of accounting, and accounting for, cuts both ways. When I started telling the story of the Ogoni struggle you will notice I suggested that our population is an estimated 500,000 and that an estimated 900 million barrels of oil have been pumped out of Ogoni. Estimates: this, to me, is one of the greatest problems facing my community. We don't actually know who we are or what we have.

I remember traveling around the wine region in the Western Cape and locking horns with a famous old wine maker, Jan Boland Coetzee. As we sat in his elegant and immaculate study, with its framed pictures of him on the cover of the New Yorker and his Springbok Rugby Shirts, he regarded me with a steely, suspicious expression while absent-mindedly tapping his shoulder with a wine thief. He explained how he could never leave South Africa like many of his contemporaries. The African sun, he reasoned poetically, had boiled his blood to all sorts of things. His family had been farming the corner of Africa we were standing on for four centuries. I looked at this grizzly old Afrikaner and reluctantly concluded that he had a point: his provenance in Africa was longer than mine, which could only be traced back two or three generations, or as far back as my then ageing grandfather's memories could be relied on. That is when I began to appreciate the historical implications for oral communities in a literate world. If any of you have read Gabriel García Márquez's *One Hundred Years of Solitude* or even Mario Vargas Liosa's *The Storyteller*, you will appreciate the power of the written, as against the oral, testimony in deciding the fate of a people.

By writing, by accounting for ourselves, the Ogoni might eventually succeed in rewriting a story that has disenfranchised them. Perhaps the most notable episode in that disenfranchisement was Nigeria's land use decree of 1978, which transferred the ownership of mineral wealth found under the territory of the Federal Republic of Nigeria to the executive government. The Ogoni Bill of Rights was an attempt to not only redress this transfer, and hold the oil companies to account, but also to enable the Ogoni people to use its resources for Ogoni development. The Bill of Rights was an instrument, a tool that was very much of the moment. And yet on further consideration it seems to me that a full reckoning and extrapolation of the Bill of Rights might occasion a redrawing of the map of Ogoni, and of Nigeria, enabling these colonial constructs to be a fully realized and functional part of a truly global world.

Ogoni must take stock of who they are, where they come from, and where they wish to go. By that I mean we must use new technologies to rewrite our history, to redraw the map. We must use advances in genetic mapping, in satellite imaging and other geodata to give a true account of our history, or our resources, so that we can actually and accurately plan for the future. Of course none of this is new. In Canada, where I now live, there are communities who are doing precisely this—building a cultural inventory as a basis for reconciling the past to a more sustainable future. In the same way I see this kind of full reckoning as the basis for what I have determined as creative justice. This means that the Ogoni can actually use this opportunity in our history to make a decisive transformation by demanding that the Federal government and the oil companies compensate us by allowing us to rebuild our communities, bottom-up, using new technologies to enable us to give informed prior consent to sustainable economic and social policies.

In short all this may mean we have to dismantle, or at least supplant, the oral traditions that have informed and built Ogoni society. It means rewriting our history to fit the needs of our future; it means we have to embrace the global future but on our own terms. It means that once again the Ogoni have to innovate. This should not alarm the traditionalists. What is now a tradition was once an innovation.

Response to Ken Wiwa, 'If this is your Land, where are your Stories?'

Adam Higazi

The Ogoni are one of numerous ethnic groups inhabiting the oil-rich Niger Delta: a floodplain in southern Nigeria covering some 25,640 km^2 with extensive wetlands ecosystems of mangrove forests and creeks. The Niger Delta is formed where the River Niger (the longest river in West Africa) flows into the Atlantic Ocean. Sedimentary deposits that have flowed down the Niger and Benue Rivers[1] over millions of years have accumulated in the delta, giving rise to a light crude oil that is highly valued by Western oil companies and refineries. Oil is the cornerstone of the Nigerian economy, with revenues now constituting about 95 per cent of the country's foreign currency earnings. Unfortunately, due to the high level of corruption and the large profit margins of the oil companies, the billions of dollars generated have only benefited a small political elite. Nigeria lacks the strong and accountable institutions necessary to facilitate a more just and democratic use of its oil resources. Oil has also led to the neglect of other areas of the economy, such as agriculture and manufacturing, turning Nigeria into a 'rentier' state, dependent on external revenue rather than local taxation. At the same time, oil companies operating in the Niger Delta, such as Shell and Chevron, have not adhered to environmental standards that they would be forced by law to meet in Western countries. Such laws do exist in Nigeria, but they are not enforced—oil is extracted with scant regard for local populations and laws are routinely flouted.

The majority of Nigerians live in poverty, eking out a living in overcrowded and polluted urban conditions or subsisting in rural areas. According to the 2007 UN Human Development Report, life expectancy at birth in Nigeria is only 46.5 years, and the country ranked 158th out of 177 in the human development index (a multi-dimensional measure of living standards). Nigeria has a much larger population than any other African country—no one knows the exact figure, but the 2006 census claimed 140 million. There are also between 300 and 400 ethnic groups in the country, which is also one of the most linguistically diverse in the world. There are more poor people in Nigeria than in any other African country, but worse still the standard of living measured by human development is lower than the sub-Saharan African average. Essential services and amenities such as hospitals, schools, clean water, roads, and electricity are absent or deficient in large areas of the country, including the Niger Delta. Rural areas generally tend to be most lacking in facilities, but as well as neglect the people of the Niger Delta have been severely harmed by oil production—through the undermining of their traditional livelihoods of farming and fishing due to oil spillages and pollution, the brutal repression they have faced from the state's security apparatus, and the selfish interests and incompetence of their political representatives and traditional leaders.

It is within this context that the struggle of the Ogoni and other peoples of the Niger Delta needs to be interpreted. The Ogoni are one of many populations negatively affected by oil production in the delta. There had been protests and non-violent 'direct action' against oil companies in the past, but the Ogoni were the first to launch an organized and concerted mass movement. Their non-violent protests were directed against Shell Oil[2] and successive Nigerian military regimes—this generated international publicity and support for their cause. The international support from organizations such as Greenpeace and the Body Shop was well-meaning, but adopted single issue narratives, notably of an 'indigenous' peoples' struggle against the decimation of their environment, whereas in fact the political reality was far more complex. At the centre of the struggle was Ken Saro-Wiwa, a respected writer and activist who was instrumental in founding MOSOP—the Movement for the Survival of the Ogoni People—in 1990. The Ogoni Bill of Rights issued by MOSOP in the same year demanded political autonomy within Nigeria for the Ogoni: the right to control their land and benefit from a fair share of the economic resources derived from it, to use and develop their languages, and to protect their oil-producing environment from further devastation.[3] MOSOP campaigned against Shell's appalling environmental record in Ogoni, including its failure to clean up or compensate for oil spills that polluted fishing waters and farmland—the mainstay of people's livelihoods in the Niger Delta. It also opposed the laying of seismic lines and oil pipelines through villages, farmland, and forests, and the huge disruption caused by gas flaring—the burning of unused gas into the atmosphere, causing incessant light and noise pollution. At the local level, the enormous volumes of greenhouse gases flared in the Niger Delta are said to cause acid rain, eroding buildings and poisoning water sources.

In November 1992 MOSOP 'issued a thirty-day ultimatum to all the oil companies operating on their land—Shell, Chevron, and NNPC [Nigerian National Petroleum Corporation]—to pay back-rents and royalties and also compensation for land devastated by oil exploration and production activities, or leave.'[4] The oil companies ignored MOSOP's demands, but Saro-Wiwa ratcheted up the campaign, linking human and environmental rights, and in the process turned MOSOP into a mass, non-violent protest movement. A rally on 4 January 1993 was said to have been attended by hundreds of thousands of Ogoni, timed to coincide with the start of the United Nations Year of indigenous People.[5] Saro-Wiwa gained the support of prominent environmental and human rights groups in the West and MOSOP became a thorn in the side of the Nigerian junta and Shell. The Nigerian military responded with repression and violence, especially under General Sani Abacha, who came to power in a coup in 1993 and ruled as a dictator until his death in 1998. Soldiers were dispatched to destroy Ogoni villages and shoot villagers on sight. Non-violent protests against Shell facilities were put down with brutal force. Accusations abound that Shell was not only aware of the repression but had close links with the military who it called in to 'protect' its installations.

Thousands of Niger Delta people are estimated to have been killed in the protracted military crackdown under Abacha.[6] The Ogoni, however, were hampered by a divided leadership, some of which supported the federal government and received patronage from oil companies, while Sara-Wiwa and others had more popular legitimacy and had become isolated from the government. Shell suspended operations in Ogoni in 1993, but in 1995 Ken Saro-Wiwa and eight fellow

Ogoni activists were falsely accused of murdering four Ogoni elders and made to stand trial in a kangaroo court. The trial was strongly condemned by international observers and Nigerian human rights activists. Western and other African leaders called for 'clemency', but failed to condemn the trial in strong terms or put serious pressure on Nigeria's military government (which was indifferent to external criticism). The Ogoni activists were hanged on 10 November 1995, during the meeting of Commonwealth Heads of State in Auckland. MOSOP disintegrated and the Abacha government, aided by the oil companies, launched a smear campaign against Saro-Wiwa.

What does this recent tragic history tell us about land rights and the present insurgency in the Niger Delta? Ken Saro-Wiwa wrote, in his pre-conviction statement, 'I predict that a denouement of the riddle of the Niger Delta will soon come. The agenda is being set for this trial. Whether the peaceful ways favoured will prevail depends on what the oppressor decides, what signals it sends out to the waiting public.'[7] Saro-Wiwa's words were prescient because the rebellion subsequently spread across the delta, promulgated especially by the Ijaw—the largest ethnic group in the Niger Delta. On 11 December 1998, shortly before the return to civilian rule in Nigeria, Ijaw youths and political representatives from some 40 clans met in the town of Kaiama, Bayelsa State, and issued the Kaiama Declaration—'a ten-point statement demanding that all oil companies leave "Ijaw land" by 30 December 1998, pending the resolution by the Nigerian federal government of questions relating to the ownership and control of petroleum resources and political autonomy for the Ijaw.'[8] This was followed by protest marches and demonstrations across the Niger Delta in late 1998 and early 1999—met with a brutal response by the military regime of General Abdulsalami Abubakar, in which an estimated 200 people were killed.[9]

The Ijaw Youth Council (IYC) emerged out of the NGO Environmental Rights Action, and was established to realize the goals of the Kaiama Declaration. Several of its leaders had already been active in campaigning on behalf of MOSOP, and the declaration was modelled on the Ogoni Bill of Rights.[10] The IYC sought 'to create a popular mass movement out of disparate episodes of "uprising" . . . and to unite the culturally diverse groups that make up the Ijaw people under a single ethnic umbrella.'[11] Prior to the establishment of the IYC there were several other youth-led civic groups that had campaigned on a more local basis. In the wake of the state's violent response to the Kaiama Declaration, and due to the influence of Niger Delta politicians who sought to weaken the IYC, the leadership split into two factions—the IYC and the Niger Delta Peoples Volunteer Force, which declared 'that the peaceful methods of the IYC had not been effective and that what the new civilian government headed by President Obasanjo would heed was military action. Even so, the bulk of the remaining IYC members continued on the path of non-violent political action.'[12] The NDPVF disrupted oil production, but much of the trouble has been sponsored by high profile Niger Delta politicians and elites who have in the process enriched themselves: bunkering oil (stealing oil from the pipelines—often on a huge scale) and diverting government funds meant for development. Such armed groups may have emerged on the basis of oppression and justifiable grievances, but the fact is they are now criminal gangs, often serving the interests of rich elites.[13]

The federal government has been brutal in its responses to the insecurity, and its legitimacy compromised as high-level politicians, even from outside the delta, have made millions from oil bunkering. A major escalation occurred in February 2006, when government helicopter gun ships attacked an Ijaw village in the western delta, ostensibly to stop oil bunkering. This seems to have been the immediate trigger for the formation of the Movement for the Emancipation of the Niger Delta (MEND)—currently the most notorious militia in the delta. But as Ike Okonta points out, 'MEND is not so much an "organisation" but an idea in which many civic, communal, and political groups, each with its own local specificity and grievances, have bought into.'[14] Dozens of oil workers have been kidnapped by groups under the MEND label—though they are almost always released unharmed after the necessary publicity (and ransom) has been gained (although the government and oil companies always deny that ransoms are paid). At the height of their assaults MEND shut down a quarter of Nigeria's oil production.

How do the conflicts in the Niger Delta relate to what is happening elsewhere in the country? Nigerian politics is above all about resource control and access to federal government allocations, derived from oil revenues, made to states and local governments. Petroleum Decree No. 51 of 1969 and the 1978 Land Use Decree directed oil revenues to the federal government rather than the oil producing states and gave the government direct control of customary land. There are now 36 states and 774 local government areas in the federation competing for their share of federal government revenues. There is a revenue-allocation formula, which in fact does allow oil-producing states a greater share (15 per cent) of oil money than other states, but this is not perceived as adequate by people in the Niger Delta, and due to the mismanagement of funds has not redressed the deep-seated social and environmental problems in the area. The conflict is therefore partly one between national and local control of resources. While groups in the Niger Delta want more control over the resources being extracted from their land, elsewhere in Nigeria such demands are not usually given a sympathetic hearing. In northern Nigeria—the region I am more familiar with—oil tends to be seen as part of the country's national endowment rather than the preserve of people in the Niger Delta. One academic even made the argument that the oil does not belong exclusively to the people of the Niger Delta, because the sediments through which the oil formed flowed down the Niger and Benue Rivers which run a course through northern Nigeria! At the same time, ethnic consciousness has increased across Nigeria in recent years, with intense poverty fuelling resource conflicts across the country. It is encouraging that in response to the external pressures of economic and social change—which threaten many smaller cultures with extinction—oral histories and languages are increasingly being recorded. Such projects are, however, enmeshed with quests for land rights and resources. Histories are used politically and are at times manipulated to define land ownership and establish cohesion among ethnic groups that were previously fractionalized along clan or territorial lines. Ethnic mobilization occurs for different reasons: as part of a struggle against governments, corporations, and other ethnic groups for resource control. The struggle for human rights, justice, and the environment is of real importance in the Niger Delta, as Saro-Wiwa demonstrated, but such principles have too often been undermined by the failings of local politics and the selfish interests of elites.

5

Whose World is it Anyway?

Richard Leakey

I accepted to speak tonight, on the question of 'Whose world is it anyway?', in a weak moment. I have since reflected on what it was that led me to embrace the unenviable task of speaking out on a topic to which, in many respects, I myself have very few legitimate rights. Perhaps it was the thought of trying out some ideas, provoking some discussion. I would leave some people with questions, some with answers and others, undoubtedly, furious. Whichever constituency you will eventually feel to be yours, I ask you to remember that I am only one person. I no longer hold any public posts and so pose relatively little threat to those who have coveted positions in public life. I can, if you like, be dismissed as a has-been of no consequence. So I hope you will allow me to lead with my chin.

The central question tonight is land ownership. Having worked in a variety of different roles, and finally in a government position as Secretary to the Cabinet and Head of the Civil Service, I can tell you that there is little that is more critical, more immediate, and more problematic than land in my country, Kenya. The range of opinions, of ideas, and above all the range of certainties that exists on land issues is bewildering. It is not unknown for a number of these different—and sometimes contradictory—positions to inhabit a single individual all at the same time. Above all stands the central belief that when it comes it to land, you can and must have a position.

My own position was made public relatively recently, and in a rather extraordinary set of circumstances. I had been unexpectedly invited to South Africa to attend a meeting of the World Parks Congress, a gathering of all the National Parks Wardens and Leaders, the IUCN, and various other agencies concerned with setting aside land for public means. I was to be a participant in a particular panel, and looked forward to raising some important—or at least to me important—questions at the meeting. When I arrived I remember being impressed by the programme, impressed by the list of people who were to speak, and impressed by the summaries of speeches that were to be given. So imagine my surprise when somebody who was not listed as a participant, and who unconnected with any official programme, suddenly appeared from nowhere and was invited to give what appeared to be a keynote policy speech on the rights of indigenous people. This lady, as it happens, was from Central America; she was dressed in what I took to be traditional clothing. Highly articulate, though speaking in Spanish rather than English or in her own language, she proceeded to describe a totally unacceptable position where the *indigeni* or the indigenous people of the world have been denied, and had their rights stolen from them. The way forward for the World Parks Congress, she went on, was to recognize the illegality of actions over the historical period and for retribution to be arranged in the sense, at least as far as our meeting was concerned, of returning all of the protected areas—that is the national parks, the game reserves, and national forests—back to the indigenous people, who would of course look after them very well indeed. We, meanwhile, should move out and move off. This was stolen land that we were talking about. There was to be no more nonsense. Her remarks received a tremendous round of applause.

Now, I am one of those minorities that is not indigenous anywhere—of which more later—and so as a minority I exercised my minority right to feel some consternation at the sight of people who appear, as if from nowhere, and begin to speak for others. I found myself sitting on the podium wondering what on earth had happened. There was clearly a political dimension to what was going on. The chairperson of the meeting was deeply concerned, it seemed to me, not to irritate this lady. I also noticed that in the hall at the time there were a number of other people (I should have noticed this before) wearing blankets and holding clubs—Maasai, claiming to be the representatives of the indigenous people of East Africa and various other groups who claimed to be indigenous. What was happening? When it came to the discussion I said, perhaps somewhat rashly, that I honestly did not know what this question of indigenous peoples' rights was all about. I got into deep trouble. People booed and hissed. I was declared to be an enemy of the people. I was threatened. The press carried articles saying that I had been the one negative element in this entire meeting, which was so well founded and so positive, that I had cast a spanner in the works. But all I had asked was what it means to be indigenous. What does that word actually mean? Now my friends said that I was not as innocent as I appeared. Maybe that is true. That is part of being a public speaker. In any event, I have since given a lot of thought to this extremely complicated subject. And as a result of that complexity, and no doubt too of some remarks I have made in different places at different times, the organizers of this particular series thought it might be appropriate, or at least entertaining, to have me come and get into trouble in Oxford. Not too much trouble, I hope.

To return to my question that day, what does the word 'indigenous' mean? When it comes to Africa, the question needs to be set within the context of colonialism. In a country like Kenya, which has a very well documented colonial past (though not necessarily a well documented interpretation of that colonial past), colonialism started when the British arrived, for a variety of reasons—some of which were positive, some less so. Among the more positive motives, still not always believed but nonetheless a factor at the time, was the British Government's involvement in an attempt to stop slavery. Previous to the British Government, British nationals had been to Kenya to trade. There they had found nationals of other parts of the world, although there were no passports at that time, trading in a variety of goods—some in ivory, some in people. The trade in people was not uncommon in the northern parts of Kenya and indeed Kenya was one of the last countries in pre-independence years to recognize that slavery had not properly ceased and that there were still holdings in the north where slavery was common. Be that as it may, colonialism was in part to do with setting up a state that would oppose the practice, even if many citizens of today's Kenya, including myself, are surprised and disgusted that slavery lasted as long as it did.

Of course, the first colonizers were obviously concerned with much more than slavery and here we come to some of the less positive aspects of their arrival. That 'much more' included taking land from people who did not seem to know that they owned it, and developing commerce on that land. This is when the whole issue of land ownership took root in the modern Kenya, as people began to feel that they had rights over their land. It is important to understand that these rights were not necessarily of ownership in the European sense. Nonetheless, whether you own it or you have the ownership of rights to raise it, rights to burn it, or rights to use it, these are rights that should be respected. Indeed, I think we have oversimplified the question of land in terms of rights so that these have become synonymous with absolute ownership, as offered by what are largely Western values (or at least British values), through which you acquire title and are able to use that title as collateral in a financial instrument. That particular understanding of land, and rights to it, is something that goes with colonialism and makes land peculiar in terms of its place in society more generally.

Land adjudication and land ownership, in other words, became an instrument with which those in charge were able to exercise financial, and therefore political, power. One of the most important issues was that for many years before and up to independence, you had to be of a certain colour, and of a certain status, to own land. The so-called white land—that is to say the white highlands of Kenya—became of particular value. Those who owned it established farms; meanwhile other people lived on land but had no rights. In Kenya today there still exist tracts of land inhabited by families who can trace their lineage back at least six hundred years. *Six hundred years.* Inhabited, though, not owned: the modern Kenyan government, in all its erudite class of sophisticated posturing, considers them squatters. For instance, on the island of Lamu in north Kenya, where I own some property, if you are an upcountry person you have been able to and still can obtain land. If, on the other hand, you are a Lamu person who has four or five hundred years of history, you are not able to acquire title to the land on which you live. Again, you are thought to be squatting, which means the government has certain rights to evict you from your home. And all this, remember, a full thirty-five years after independence. The problem in that specific case is that the people who have sat on this land for five or six hundred years have Islamic-sounding names. They also have Islamic beliefs, and as a result of those beliefs, or rather the prejudice against them, are refused all applications to land title on Lamu. In this way the wrongs that were initiated during the colonial era, however you define that era, have persisted all the way through to 2005. It is hardly surprising that land ownership has become an extremely emotive issue.

I suppose connected to these issues is another question which interests me as an individual: the question of indigenous rights. Earlier on I made a passing swipe to the effect that I was not indigenous to anywhere. I would desperately like to be indigenous but I do not know where I will find a place that would accept me as an indigene. I have a passport that belongs to Kenya; I speak my mother tongue which is Swahili; I will give my life for my country; but I am not an indigenous Kenyan. Neither am I an indigene of this country. If I try to come to Britain I have to produce evidence as to why I should be given a visa. This gets more difficult as time goes by. The same applies in other parts of the world. Indeed you could say that I am really not very welcome wherever I go. Most of the time, this does not worry me unduly: I have been very privileged, and as a privileged person there are ways of rising above such things—old boy networks, personal loyalties and alliances, things of that kind. But it is not really the same, is it? No rights to a visa, and a citizenship in Kenya which could be removed at any time: the thought of this, and the unfairness of it, has kept me awake from time to time.

So if I cannot be indigenous, who can? What is the cut-off for indigenousness? I see people of African descent who are considered in all their rights as indigenous to America. I see people descended from all kinds of nationalities indigenous in Britain, where it is also possible, post-devolution, to find the Scottish now saying that they are indigenous in one part of the island and others are not. In Africa, and more especially in Kenya, there has been population mobility for a long time, so that the origins of its present inhabitants is one of the great mysteries. You look at the agrarian society around Mount Kenya, or you look at the pastoralist society in the Maasai steppe, and you can safely suppose that they have indeed been here a long time: pastoralist cattle came into the country several hundred, several thousand years ago, and you can probably trace them back to Central Africa or North Africa. But this is just the point. As far as we can tell, all the people in Kenya came to Kenya at one point or another. The original occupants of the space called Kenya are not there; they got pushed out by somebody, at some point, somewhere else. Now, it is not the purpose of this evening's lecture to document who got pushed out when, and why, but rather to pose the question of when 'indigenous' begins?

Similar kinds of issues are raised in conservations where the wish is sometimes expressed that a national park be created in order to maintain a certain area in its pristine—in the sense of original—nature. But when was the original nature in the national park? Was it when it was first documented as a national park, which may have been a bad year with a lot of drought, or was it pristine when there was a heavy rainfall and there were no cattle? Or was it pristine when there was an early paucity of human ancestors? These kinds of questions—some more obviously ridiculous than others—remind me of a conversation that I had with President Moi. We were talking at a Cabinet meeting, when I was running the Kenya government as Secretary, and there arose the subject of corruption. One of the President's ideas for dealing with corruption had something in common with the conservationists. He said:

'Well, you know there has to be some cut-off point. We can't just prosecute everybody who has been corrupt in the past because who is there going to be left? We have to have a line in the sand and say before this you may have been corrupt but we assume the evidence has gone but after this, clearly you were corrupt.'

So I said: 'When is this? When do we draw that line?' I do not want to give you the date that he offered, but it was not fair: it plainly was not fair to some people who were not at that time in the government. And so I replied with an alternative: 'Why don't we make it as of now?' Let us not be corrupt up to today and from tomorrow we'll be corrupt if we do the same things.'

'Yes, but there are some things in the pipeline. It's very difficult to draw a line'.

This is a true story. I raise corruption because it is like being indigenous. Is it 100 years? Is it 300 years? Is it 500 years? Is it the arrival of foreign influence in the form of Islam? Is it the post-Islamic contact in the form of the arrival of the missionaries? As the late President Kenyatta said: 'For any missionary to have got off his boat he has to have been breaking all the commandments. They were a rotten lot or they wouldn't have stayed here. They have to have coveted our land, and a lot of other things too.' So you cannot put it at the arrival of the missionaries. But where do you draw this line? I have no idea. What is very clear is that if you are going to be fair, it is really very difficult to say you are indigenous and will enjoy some rights and they are not indigenous because they came a year later and have none.

So, let us go back to the conundrum that I created at the conference in Durban. Clearly in certain parts of the world, the indigenous people have largely been wiped out by invading racists. America is a case in point—North and South—where the Caucasians have wreaked havoc with almost every society and tribal system. In the United States there are very few indigenous people left, and they are eking out their existence on land that is set aside, where they have special rights. In Canada, too, there are questions about native rights, especially regarding rights to fishing and whaling. In these cases you can begin to understand why a special case is being made. In Africa, fortunately—perhaps some would say unfortunately—the indigenous people were numerous enough: there was sufficient resistance to ensure that the invading forces—Caucasians, along with other invaders from the Arabian peninsula—never gained full control. It is here that by invoking the concept of indigenousness, discussions of land issues in our country seem to me to miss the point. As I tried to remind my audience in Durban, we in Kenya have people who are not only 'indigenous', but running the country. They are smart people, well dressed, have university educations, wear suits, and drive Mercedes. And yet they are every bit as 'indigenous' as the guy raising hell at international meetings. Or, to put the same thing the other way, the Maasai warrior who comes to Durban to clap his hands when Leakey is speaking is no more indigenous than the President of Kenya, or the head of Kenya Airways. All this is not to say, then, that there has not been some grave injustices committed in different parts of the world. My claim is merely that one size does not fit all. We cannot take the position when talking about land rights that what pertains in Scotland should pertain in Brasilia, or even that what might solve a problem in one part of Africa, will come to the same thing in another. As I went on to argue in Durban, 'This is not something you want to bring to Durban. If you haven't got your rights in Kenya, if you want to change your members of parliament, if you want to change the Kenyan constitution, these are not questions for the international community. This is not a problem that you can address in the capitals of North and South.'

This brings me to the question of Kenya as a nation. Rightly or wrongly there is a country called Kenya. While I recognize that countries such as Kenya, Uganda, and Tanzania were made up of other nations at the time of independence, the fact is they have been made up: they now exist. And if we are going to have a country called Kenya, if we are going to be represented in New York at the United Nations, and if we are going to have agreements with the WTO, we have to run our country as a sovereign state. There are forty-nine different languages spoken in Kenya, and many of these would consider themselves remnants of nations. But we solve no problem if we go back to being a forty-nine-state federation. It is my view that the only way to support the nation state is to support a system of governance that reflects the complexity of Kenya's make-up and historical past while nonetheless retaining the sovereignty of that state. I think many African governments and African leaders have recognized that to tamper with the sovereignty question is to really kiss it goodbye. The implications, in terms of civil war, of going back to different nations that made up the modern states is, I think, simply unacceptable.

So what is Kenya, as a nation state, to do about land? First of all we have to recognize that land has had a particular value in some countries. In Kenya land adjudication and land ownership has been possible for some for over close to a century. It has often been used as an instrument to achieve enormous wealth, frequently at the expense of others. The inequality of access to that wealth is certainly manifest in a survey of modern Kenya. Today we are in a position where if you wish to borrow money to send your daughter to high school or university, or you have a grandmother who needs a serious operation and you need to borrow some capital (it may not be much, maybe a thousand pounds, or several hundred pounds), the only instrument you can use as collateral in securing a loan is land title. For this reason land title has taken on a very peculiar position in Kenyan society, since people have come to aspire to land ownership in a way that is totally unreal in terms of the land value. One of the ways forward is to think in terms of finding a mechanism by which people can access the economy using collateral that is not based on land ownership but is based on something else. That would be one constructive position.

Secondly, we also have to acknowledge that in countries like Kenya—and there are many others in the tropics—land ownership can be inimical to land use. The deterioration of land value through over-grazing, erosion, and loss of vegetative cover is a factor that the country, if it is a sovereign state, cannot afford to ignore. The rights to land should not include the rights to debase it. On the contrary, land has got to be looked after as a national asset because what happens on your piece of land affects people who are living miles from you who cannot afford to be degraded, as they so often are. In Kenya, it is unfortunately the case that nobody thought through these issues: most land legislation and land law in Kenya was established at a time when it was assumed that the majority would be happy to live on community land, and certainly never aspire to own it. The idea that individuals in the community would want ownership of their land arrived after independence, partly underscored by the importance of acquiring title that offers access to the financial markets through collateral. I think this is a very critical factor. In the long term it is possible that Kenya is going to have to face up to a draconian overhaul of the idea of land ownership, in such a way that it is replaced with land occupancy rights through a long- or short-term lease. For this reason I have suggested to many people who are currently involved in conservation, and who wish to buy land from disadvantaged people, that rather than buy they should lease. Why not give somebody who has a perpetual right what is effectively the same by giving them a ninety-nine year lease, or a fifty-year lease. Fifty years from now those people will be very unhappy if they find they do not own anything: much better to lease the land, get the rights to zone it, and the rights to manage what happens on it in terms of wildlife, soil erosion, or water catchment. Let us not take any more away from people who consider that the land is theirs and who are only giving in because they are in such abject poverty. Entrenched in the great civilizations of the New World was the idea that land was to be used, but never owned. I do not think it is too late to turn the clock back.

In conclusion, it is my view that being indigenous or non-indigenous and owning land, as opposed to having rights to the use of that land are equally spurious in the twenty-first century. First of all, let us not exacerbate artificial differences, a product of Western thinking through the colonial era. Let us recognize that somebody who has been in the country for 150 years is no less of a stakeholder than somebody who has been there for 300 years. Although people do not believe me and roll their eyes in despair when I say: 'We all came from Africa anyway', we are all indigenous really. We all came from the same place. Second, the use of the land is far more important than the land itself. Addressing—highly and rightly politicized—issues of access to water, protection of water catchment, and protection of resources in terms of national use and international security makes far more sense than petty arguments over title. Whose world is it anyway? It is certainly not ours.

Response to Richard Leakey, 'Whose World is it Anyway?'

Lotte Hughes

Conflicts over land are among the most hotly contested issues in Kenya today, as Dr Leakey acknowledges. It is not just a matter of 'land ownership', but equitable access to and control over natural resources such as water, pasture, forests, wildlife, and minerals. Many recent and ongoing so-called ethnic conflicts are in fact struggles over access to resources, but some people (especially politicians) prefer for political reasons to call them 'ethnic' or 'tribal'.

First, I want to briefly mention some recent developments, so that readers will understand the background to what Dr Leakey is saying. Whatever he may think about the validity of indigenous peoples' land claims (I shall define 'indigenous' in a moment), the urgent need to address land issues and resolve past injustices was acknowledged by two recent land commissions and was implicit in a proposed new constitution. Kenyans voted against the latter in a November 2005 referendum, which turned into a massive vote of no confidence in the government of President Kibaki. The draft constitution had a chapter on environment and natural resources, and another on land and property, which emphasized equitable access, the need to secure land rights, safeguard communally-held land, and settle the landless. But many people did not feel that this, and other parts of the proposed constitution, went far enough. The Orange 'No' Campaign declared in newspaper advertisements that 'marginalized groups and minorities have been completely ignored'.

Indigenous and minority groups were among those who voted 'no' en masse. They included hunter-gatherer and pastoralist communities—long-term victims of land snatching. They feared they would lose even more land if the constitution were passed, as well as control over natural resources such as wildlife. Marginalized people have to share their living space with wildlife, often at considerable cost to themselves in terms of human–animal conflict, and demand a greater share of wildlife tourism revenues and a larger role in wildlife management. Pastoralists in particular also opposed plans for a National Land Commission that would have managed public land including game parks and reserves. (In a bid to bribe the Maasai community to vote 'yes', the government promised to return Amboseli National Park to Maasai control and downgrade it to a game reserve. The community took the bribe, but still voted 'no'. Conservation groups opposed the government's plans for degazettement in the courts; so far as I know, the case is not yet resolved.) Indigenous groups also condemned proposals to allow women to inherit land, calling this 'culturally abhorrent'. Minister for Lands, Amos Kimunya, tried to allay some of these fears by saying: 'Kenyans must not be cheated that the new constitution will take away their land . . . No community will be deprived of their land'.[1] Few believed him.

The most recent government-appointed land commission produced the Ndung'u Report into illegal allocation of public land (published June 2004). It named and shamed members of the current and former governments, among other people, who benefited financially from this land grab. The report declared that ' "land crimes" are as much a part of Kenya's past wrongdoings as economic crimes and human rights crimes'. And that 'the corrupt and fraudulent practices which have bedevilled Kenya's public land allocation and administration' had gone on for 'several decades'. Every post-colonial administration is certainly guilty of corrupt land (and other) practices. At the time of writing, the Anglo-Leasing scandal, and other evidence of high-level corruption produced by Kenya's former 'anti-corruption tsar' John Githongo (now living in exile in Oxford), threaten to bring down the government.

However, the roots of the 'land crimes' problem are much older, and lie in the British colonial era. Dr Leakey does acknowledge this, when for instance he says 'the wrongs that were initiated during the colonial era . . . have persisted all the way through to 2005', and that British colonizers took 'land from people who did not seem to know that they owned it'. But these admissions sit at odds with his rejection of specific rights and claims. If the initial land grab was wrong and illegal, do the victims not have a right to challenge it, however many years later? The excuse which is often made, not least by the OAU and AU, is that any attempt to make post-colonial amends will ignite ethnic strife. Dr Leakey appears to be suggesting this, too. But as a recent report on Kenya's minorities puts it: 'Claims by particular communities are often seen as threats to the unity of the Kenyan nation, instead of opportunities to make all groups feel included and to ensure that their needs are recognized'.[2]

There is a certain lack of logic at the centre of Dr Leakey's argument, which does not add up to a coherent whole. One major contradiction is his later claim that a special case should not be made for indigenous peoples in Africa, in comparison to North America, because they were 'numerous enough' and showed 'sufficient resistance to ensure that the invading forces... never gained full control'. How does this square with the fact that (among other invaders) Britain, Germany, France, Belgium, Portugal, Italy, Spain, and Boers of Dutch descent all established colonies or protectorates on the continent? Africans certainly put up a fight, but in most places they were unable to prevent colonization and the takeover of their land. The exceptions were Ethiopia and Liberia, which remained nominally independent by 1914; it could be said that Liberia was re-colonized by African-Americans.

Indigenous Peoples

Before I go any further, I need to define the term indigenous, a word Dr Leakey claims—rather disingenuously—not to understand. It applies to aboriginal or autochthonous peoples, descended from the pre-colonial inhabitants of particular territories, who define themselves as indigenous and are regarded as such by others. It does not include the descendants of European settlers in the colonies (so that rules out Dr Leakey). Neither does it refer only to people who always occupied a certain space, or were first-comers there, because of course human beings have, from the beginning of time, ceaselessly moved about the globe (see below, 'What we can agree on'). The 'cut-off [point] for indigenousnous' which so vexes this speaker was the European conquest of overseas territories: that is 'when "indigenous" begins', according to most current definitions. So we are *not* 'all indigenous really'.

Indigenous communities are usually not socially and politically dominant within the nation state, and are often marginalized by those in power (though Fiji is a notable exception). They have distinct traditions, identities, customs and beliefs, and feel they have a special relationship with the land and natural resources, which is often fundamental to their identity and survival as distinct peoples. Although there is much disagreement over definitions, those coined by the United Nations and the International Labour Organization (ILO) have come to be widely accepted. To quote ILO Convention No. 169 (Article 1), indigenous peoples are 'tribal peoples in independent territories whose social, cultural and economic conditions distinguish them from other sections of the national community, and whose status is regulated wholly or partially by their own customs or traditions . . . ' and 'peoples in independent countries who are regarded as indigenous on account of their descent from the populations which inhabited the country, or a geographical region to which the country belongs, at the time of conquest for colonization . . . and who, irrespective of their legal status, retain some or all of their social, economic, cultural and political institutions'.[3] The numbers of people who define themselves as indigenous in Kenya make up around 20 per cent of the population of 28 million (1999 census).

When Dr Leakey says he desperately wishes he was indigenous to somewhere, he knows he is being deliberately facetious. But he is right to pose the question: who is indigenous in Africa? Arguments rage over this, with governments such as that in Botswana refusing to recognize indigenous rights on the grounds that all Africans are indigenous to the continent, so that the rights of one particular group should not be privileged over those of other citizens. Pertinent questions include: why are the Kikuyu people not considered indigenous, but the Maasai and Ogiek are? The San and Nama people of southern Africa, but not the Zulu or Ndebele? The deciding factors include whether or not the groups concerned are dominant in society or marginalized, and above all, whether their members self-identify as indigenous. Some do, some do not. (By comparison to Africa, the situation in Australia is much clearer: Aboriginal people were definitely there long before Europeans; they did not displace any pre-existing communities, so far as we know; they remain marginalized; and there are no other contenders for the indigenous title.)

As for where the *idea* of being indigenous came from, I suggest—like political consciousness—it is partly a product of imperialism itself. Anthropologists in the colonial era, working for colonial governments, classified 'native' people according to 'tribe' in order to define, control, and rule them more easily. (In fact, ethnicity is much more fluid than that, and we should no longer talk about bounded tribes at all.) By placing ethnic groups in reserves, telling people such as the Maasai that they could retain these areas for ever, and banning other 'tribes' from settling there, the British unwittingly helped to create an obsession with boundaries, 'tribal' divisions, 'tribal purity', and 'alien' intruders that is very evident in debates around indigenousness and regionalism in Kenya today. NGOs devoted to indigenous issues have also fostered an obsession with indigeneity, which can have negative effects—particularly when linked to jockeying for external funding.

This is not the place to discuss all the other complex issues around indigeneity. What I must challenge is the idea that questions about the rights of indigenous Kenyans (or anyone else) cannot be raised or discussed on an international stage. When Dr Leakey says of the issues raised in Durban that 'these are not questions for the international community', he does not seem to have grasped the fact that human rights (including those of indigenous people) are globalized in today's world.

When he declares that 'This [land rights in Kenya] is not a problem that you can address in the capitals of North and South', his argument echoes that used by defenders of President Robert Mugabe: that Zimbabwe's problems are internal to the country and no one else's business. The globalization of human rights knows no boundaries, and it should be possible to seek justice, and raise awareness of violations, at home or abroad.

Who is to Blame?

All blame for the current land crisis cannot be laid at the door of the British, who ruled Kenya in one form or another from 1895 to 1963. But their culpability cannot be ignored, as Dr Leakey appears to wish in some parts of this lecture. So let us start with a history lesson, for his historical references are sketchy and partial, as well as contradictory. It seems odd for a palaeontologist not to have a better grasp of history; maybe he is more comfortable with ancient, silent bones than angry indigenes 'wearing blankets and holding clubs'. In fact, the specific grievance he mentions (Maasai land losses at British hands, an issue raised at the World Parks Congress) is substantially valid. It has been percolating for 100 years, and there is a great deal of archival and oral evidence to support it. And guess who saw it coming? Not activists, lefties, aboriginals, loud women, or any of the people whom Dr Leakey appears to deride. In 1904, very senior British officials in what was then British East Africa warned the Colonial Office that there would be trouble if the government took the Maasai's best land and gave it to European settlers.

Administrator Charles Hobley, then Assistant Deputy Commissioner of the protectorate, cautioned: 'Maasai rights [to the Rift Valley] are a very real thing'. He became Acting Commissioner later that year—the highest post in the land—after Commissioner Sir Charles Eliot was forced to resign over promises of land grants to white farmers. Hobley said the Maasai should be compensated for being deprived of their prime Rift Valley grazing, but this never happened. Deputy Commissioner Frederick Jackson (later governor of Uganda) had told his superiors in 1903 not to 'commit a gross injustice on the Maasai' by giving in to settler claims to the Rift Valley. A year later, he again advised the Colonial Office: 'The Maasai will never give us serious trouble so long as we treat them fairly and do not deprive them of their best and favourite grazing grounds'.[4] He was overruled.

Some of these officials later went along with the land snatch, while making clear they did not agree with the way it was done. Other lower-ranking administrators such as Stephen Bagge and Arthur Collyer also spoke out in support of Maasai land rights; their voices were silenced, their careers quietly crushed. Government medical officer Dr Norman Leys was transferred to Nyasaland for opposing the Maasai moves of 1911-13, when thousands of people were forced at gunpoint from one reserve to another. It is generally acknowledged that the Maasai lost more land to the British than any other ethnic group in Kenya—an estimated 50 to 70 per cent of the land they had once occupied. But many other communities also lost out. So although I focus upon the Maasai here (largely because Dr Leakey chose this example, one I happen to know something about), I do not mean to ignore the grievances of others. Virtually every East African community suffered land and resource losses. After the British Crown decided that it owned all so-called unalienated land (that which had not been granted to settlers, syndicates, missionaries, or other Europeans), Africans became 'tenants at will of the Crown'—forced to become squatters and labourers upon land they considered theirs. Some communities, such as the Maasai and Kikuyu, were pushed into reserves. Unfortunately, they did not have written land titles and could not prove what they owned. Why would they? Concepts of land ownership and management were utterly different from European ones, and were open to European abuse. The Maasai held and managed land collectively, for example, and did not regard this as 'ownership' per se—though they have changed their tune now, of course, because property is viewed differently today. The Crown regarded as 'waste' land not in permanent African occupation and use, and confiscated it, thereby causing particular hardship to nomadic stock-keepers and hunter-gatherers who moved seasonally from one place to another.

Dr Leakey rejects 'the idea of [private] land ownership' in favour of leasehold. Yet it was the British introduction of individualized land tenure that led inexorably to today's situation, in which everyone is chasing individual titles, even if it means dividing land up into uselessly small plots—a trend he mentions. But how would he react if someone decided to take his land away from him? Is he willing to share it, which is presumably what would happen if his advice was followed, the clock was turned back, and land was simply used, not owned outright? Would he happily swap freehold for leasehold? Or is there to be one law for the privileged few and another for the masses? Furthermore, can he prove that land owned by the Leakey family—some of it apparently in former Maasai territory—was originally acquired through the 'willing buyer, willing seller' system? If not, he cannot talk so blithely. There were few professional surveyors in the early days, so some of the early land grants were acquired after prospective European settlers did their own surveying and simply told administrators what plots they'd taken. Rents for leasehold varied from a halfpenny to tuppence an acre, while most of the freehold grants before 1912 were given without any payment. I am not accusing the Leakeys of acquiring land illegally, but they—and all other large landowners, particularly those of European descent—ought to know *how* it was acquired in the first place.

Illiterate Africans had no idea what they were losing. It was only with the rise of literacy, class formation, and growing political consciousness—all direct results of colonialism, mission schools, and European colonizers' larger mission to 'improve' and 'civilize' Africans—that the victims of this daylight robbery began to question what had happened. No one need be surprised that anger resulted, and that the ball began rolling inexorably towards African rule. The anger remains undiminished, because this unfinished business could not be fully resolved at independence or afterwards. African elites took control and consolidated their gains over the next 40 years, thereby perpetuating injustice, marginalization, and inequality—and, some say, deepening it.

What we can Agree on

Dr Leakey is right to make the points about population mobility and displacement. The story of global human society is one of repeated movement and displacement. And 'rights to land should not include the rights to debase it'. For example, the Mau Forests, a vital water catchment area, are being wrecked by settlement and cultivation—much of it illegal. It is also true that it is very difficult, and probably unwise, for communities to try and prove their connectivity over time to particular tracts of land, and turn those areas into ethnic enclaves (which is what he is presumably hinting at when he says 'we solve no problem if we go back to being a forty-nine-state federation'). The Maasai, for example, are relative newcomers to Kenya compared to Ogiek and other hunter-gatherer groups who have lived in the highland forests for centuries. If anyone is, they may be 'the original occupants of the space called Kenya'—though forest dwellers did not occupy the whole territory, which was not entirely covered by woodland.

The points he goes on to make about 'pristine' environments are also correct; no one knows what 'wilderness' areas originally looked like. Human beings and animals, both domestic and wild, have helped to shape what many people wrongly regard as pristine wilderness today. I can even agree with him about indigeneity, to some extent. Further to what I have already said, it is undoubtedly a problematic concept, which is being manipulated by politicians and others for ends that are sometimes divisive and elitist.

But in conclusion I believe it is plain wrong to dismiss, from a position of self-confessed privilege and land ownership, 'petty arguments aver [land] title' as if they are so many flies to be swatted. The question remains that I posed on the day of the lecture: how would you like it (land grabbing) if it happened to you? Ten years later, a hundred years later, you would be unlikely to forget land dispossession of such magnitude, which took place in such a brutal manner, and affected so many people. Whether you like it or not, these are issues arising from colonial legacies, compounded by post-colonial governments, that must be resolved sooner rather than later. The public good, and future well-being and peace of the nation, depends on it.

6

Strategies of the Poor and some Problems of Land Reform in the Eastern Cape, South Africa: an Argument against Recommunalization

William Beinart

Most agree that land reform in southern Africa is a central, and often emotive, political and economic issue. This was the only part of sub-saharan Africa where whites, or settlers, managed to establish themselves in some numbers and appropriate large areas of agricultural land—about 40–50 per cent in Zimbabwe and Namibia; about 75 per cent in South Africa. Restoration of land was consequently an important element in the liberation struggles of the later decades of the twentieth century. Twenty years after independence in Zimbabwe, in 2000, the unresolved legacies of land politics exploded in government sponsored reoccupations that attracted global attention. While Zimbabwe's gradualist, and reasonably successful, land reform programme up to the late 1990s was achieved without loss of production, the subsequent coerced, fast-track, redistribution precipitated a major economic decline.

My talk is based on personal experience of land reform debates, planning, and processes in the 1990s in the Eastern Cape province of South Africa. The analysis was developed before the Zimbabwean crisis, but it has been reinforced by my understanding of the outcome of post-2000 fast-track land reform. I start from the assumption that access to agricultural land is not a basic human right and that the demography of South Africa precludes it. Access to residential land and shelter is, however, essential. I would like to address questions of gradualism, but my central focus will be on a less commonly rehearsed problem. While most agree that landholding should be deracialized in South Africa, the question arises as to the type of tenure that should be pursued. Most agricultural land is held by whites in the form of large commercial farms. Should these be retained, should they be subdivided into privately owned smallholdings, or should the land be re-communalized? Communal forms of land tenure are long established in South Africa, based on modified African customary systems, and remain widespread in the former African reserves or homelands. During the 1990s, land taken over by African communities in the Eastern Cape was reverting to some form of communal tenure. I went into land reform research as a historian of the rural Eastern Cape, who was well aware that peasant or small holder production, often on communally owned land, had been successful in the past. But I became increasingly convinced that recommunalization—while some would inevitably take place—was not the best solution to the complex problems of land reform. My talk tries to explain why on the basis of a specific historical case.

The Border Rural Committee (BRC), one of the leading land NGOs, played a key role in land reform planning in the Eastern Cape. In the 1980s, the BRC represented rural African communities threatened with removal under apartheid legislation. In the early 1990s, it turned its attention also to land reform and rural development, and a research group was assembled for about two years partly in order to provide information and strategies towards this end.[1] The researchers were not all in agreement about recommendations and policy, but all felt that it was important to take into account the strategies of poor people—notably the settlement, land use, and pastoral patterns adopted in areas recently occupied by Africans. These are the main focus of the paper. It is appropriate to reflect back now on that period, especially in the light of information that emerged from later research on land use in areas transferred to African ownership, and also in the light of subsequent changes in land reform policy at a national level, from 1999.

In discussions of land reform in South Africa a distinction has generally been made between the policies of restitution and redistribution. The Restitution of Land Rights Act No 22 of 1994 established legal processes through which individuals and communities could claim land that they believed was lost due to discriminatory legislation since 1913. Redistribution, by contrast, was pursued as an administrative process shaped largely by imperatives of equity. By 1995, the major vehicles for state-sponsored redistribution were the pilot land reform schemes, one in each of the nine provinces. Developed by the Ministry of Land Affairs in consultation with NGOs and land lobbies, they were to be run centrally as a national programme, and guided in each province by a secretariat responsible to an interdepartmental steering committee. About R316 m was made available nationally or R35 m for each province.[2] The schemes were envisaged not simply as land purchase programmes but as attempts at rural 'reconstruction and development'.

Provincial pilot budgets reflected this approach in that 53 per cent of expenditure was reserved for infrastructure, housing, and basic needs with only 29 per cent (R10 m) for land acquisition. The constitutional settlement reached in 1994 enshrined private property where it already existed; all land for such schemes had to be purchased from 'willing sellers'. Given that farmers were asking between about R700 and R1,000 per hectare in the Eastern Cape pilot area around the major urban centre of Queenstown at the time, the projects had to be conceived with a maximum of about 12,000 ha. in mind.[3]

Whereas restitution rested on proving legal rights, without regard to economic status, and could benefit black property owners who may have been relatively privileged, the pilots were announced as a scheme for the poor. The manual distributed noted that 'the Programme is part of a rural development strategy to address poverty and introduce equitable access to the land market. It is aimed specifically at the poor—access to land must break their poverty . . . It must reach the poorest members of the community'.[4] Special emphasis was placed upon the needs of rural women. The Department decided that the scheme would operate, at least notionally, by providing resources to individual beneficiaries, although in the majority of cases benefits would be pooled and channelled to groups. The maximum amount which any individual could receive in grants would be R15,000.

The Politics of Land in the Pilot Scheme Area

The northern section of the Border Corridor around Queenstown was chosen for the Eastern Cape pilot project partly because land struggles there were highly politicized and partly because the politicized communities had good links with the BRC. This area had suffered under the apartheid government's attempt to balkanize the country into separate African homelands. It was divided politically for some decades between three different authorities—South Africa, the Ciskei, and the Transkei. The land reform project was also intended to reintegrate policy-making for this district. It was the site of some notorious and impoverished dense settlements, notably Thornhill, Sada, and Zweledinga, which arose from forced removals, internal migrations, and apartheid planning.[5] (Dense settlements in South Africa refer to those of urban density sited in rural areas with few of the services and benefits of cities or towns.) These attracted international attention during the apartheid era, and the transition to democracy did not remove them. Partly because of the political tensions, some white farmers were keen to move out, so that there was a good deal of local land for sale. Under South Africa's willing-seller rules, this was an important criterion for land reform. Government departments and NGOs had been engaged with communities in the area over a long period and their plight was widely publicized. Most of the agencies involved could agree that it was a deserving area for investment of some kind.

By the early 1990s, Queenstown was at the epicentre of an arc of urban and dense settlement. One estimate of the population of Queenstown itself, with its townships and Ezibeleni, was 190,000 people. Ilinge, within the former Transkei, housed perhaps 20,000 people, largely former farmworkers. All of these settlements were recipients of families moving off commercial farms. Zweledinga included an estimated 35,000 people in a number of sizeable villages. Sada, Shiloh, Dongwe, and Whittlesea, increasingly one urban complex, probably housed over 60,000 people. Thornhill had declined in size to perhaps 10,000.[6] An estimated 30,000–40,000 people moved there from Herschel and the farmlands in the late 1970s.[7] But many dispersed over the c.46,000 ha. of the northern Ciskei purchased for them, or moved to Queenstown or, as will be illustrated, to state land in RA (Released Area) 60.[8]

Thus land reform was being pursued on a maximum of 12,000 ha., surrounded by a population, some of it recently rural, and hence likely to be interested in land, of around 300,000. The farming zone bordering the arc was more sparsely populated. Bisected by the 500 mm rainfall line, it is largely a sheep and cattle farming area, although there are significant pockets of irrigated agriculture and dairy production. Farms averaged around 1,000 ha. and typically housed a white farmer's family and 5 to 10 African farmworker families.[9] Any land reform would also have to take account of the farmworkers. The research team was looking, optimistically, at the purchase of 12–15 farms, depending on their size and cost. It was clear that there would be proportionately few beneficiaries of land reform.

This was not an untypical scenario in South Africa. And as in other parts of the country, the right to new land was hotly disputed. Queenstown district became a major centre for settler pastoral farmers after conquest was completed in the 1850s. However, pockets of black settlement remained, especially around mission stations such as Kamastone, Oxkraal, and Shiloh. Following the 1936 Native Land and Trust Act, the state made provision to extend the African reserved areas around these established African settlements. Systematic land purchase was delayed until the 1960s and 1970s when the Ciskei was consolidated as a homeland. The South African state felt that it was essential to establish this homeland as a contiguous geographical zones if it was to be a viable independent state. The northern Ciskeian district of Hewu consisted mainly of land purchased at this time from white commercial farmers—certainly more than 100,000 ha. Most of this land was allocated under forms of customary or communal tenure.

These old-established local communities did occupy some of the newly available farmland in Hewu. However, the purchase of this land to consolidate the Ciskei coincided with the arrival of about 18,000 people from Glen Grey and 30,000 from Herschel, districts which were being incorporated into the independent Transkei. They moved in 1976 because they wished to stay in South Africa, and retain South African citizenship. At that stage, the Ciskei had not opted for independence. Herschel in particular was a severely congested and eroded district so the possibility of new land in Hewu was attractive. When they arrived, the immigrants experienced dire conditions at the transit camps of Zweledinga and Thornhill, but they were not entirely without success in the competition for new land. Much of RA (released area) 59 around Zweledinga was transferred to Glen Grey settlers. As mentioned, some Herschel settlers moved from Thornhill to newly purchased farms in the 1980s.

Nevertheless, remaining sections of both the Herschel and Glen Grey immigrants, as well as the old-established Hewu communities, all of their numbers swollen by former farmworkers, felt that they were owed land. Their attention was focussed on Released Area 60, of about 14,000 ha. purchased by the state in the late 1970s but not allocated, partly because of indecision as to who should benefit from it. RA 60 was leased out to white farmers for most of the 1980s. The South African government then decided in the late 1980s to keep this area out of the Ciskei, and divide it into small commercial farms for black owners; surveying and fencing began. This was an interesting recognition of the coming political changes, and the beginning of a major shift in policy, away from homeland consolidation, and towards finding space for black commercial farmers within the boundaries of South Africa. But in 1991, when the political balance in the country was shifting rapidly, the neighbouring black communities forcibly occupied about 12,000 ha. of RA 60. This was part of a nationwide phenomenon, especially but not only near urban centres. It was one of the largest and best publicized land invasions in the country in the years of the transition.

The occupation of RA 60 began as part of a popular struggle for land by people from Herschel settled in Thornhill who had not been earlier beneficiaries of state land purchase.[10] It was led by dissidents in Thornhill who opposed the Ciskeian government and were absorbed in civic associations, the United Democratic Front and the ANC. They established their main settlement on the farm Merino Walk, part of RA 60, in 1991. This alarmed people in the older settlements in Hewu district and very rapidly they established three other villages on RA 60. The largest of these was named Tambo village to acknowledge the former secretary-general of the ANC in exile. The momentum for occupation grew because communities did not want to lose out in the competition for new land. Despite their illegality, strictly speaking the settlements were recognized by the state, as were some others before the 1994 election. The groups involved, with the assistance of a white manager retained by the South African Department of Agriculture, organized themselves into four main villages rather than the more traditional scattered settlements. All the new settlements in the northern Ciskei, established in the 1970s and 1980s, had conformed to the state-imposed pattern of a 'trust' village but in this case the communities chose the physical layout themselves.

By April 1995, a count of structures suggested that 2,000 people had claimed land.[11] By this time Operation Hunger, an important charity working in the area, found that the civic or residents' committee in Tambo village alone had allocated all but six of the 779 sites which they had demarcated (roughly 50 m × 50 m) and there was a strong demand for additional places.[12] If this figure is correct, it is likely that there were already more than 2,000 households in the four main villages on RA 60.[13] The occupation of RA 60, one of the major rural land invasions in the Eastern Cape, raised further the political profile of these communities and the area was visited not only by senior officials but by the new Minister of Land Affairs, Derek Hanekom, in 1994–5.

Strategies of the Poor and Land Occupation

Political claims for land were by no means the only impulse behind the occupation: it is important to examine economic forces which encouraged such large and rapid movement from existing dense settlements into new ones—a process of dispersal of dense settlement. The first point to make is that land was free on RA 60 at least until 1995, and it was also free of control by homeland Tribal Authorities or by white farmers. Secondly, a major attraction of the new RA 60 settlements was their location—strung out along the R67 main tarred road between Whittlesea and Queenstown. People put a premium on mobility and ease of access to shops, informal sector opportunities, employment, and services. They were now closer to good minibus taxi routes to Queenstown, by far the largest local centre of employment.

Thirdly, natural resources were better on RA 60 than in the Ciskei itself. Thornhill, where perhaps 30,000 people moved in the late 1970s, has often been cited as an example of how rapidly large concentrations of people, without adequate services, can denude vegetation and exhaust other natural resources.[14] Similarly, both fuelwood and pastures close to the major settlements along the eastern boundary of the Ciskei, around Sada, Zweledinga, and Whittlesea became sparse. Even in areas where there were urban services, such as Sada, accommodation was in short supply with many living in shacks or back rooms.[15] There was a strong incentive for people there to find a site on which to construct their own shelter. Former white-owned farms across the fence in RA 60 were part of the same ecological zone, but had richer firewood and grazing resources. Most had a good cover of *Acacia karoo* for firewood and goat browse.[16] Lack of water provision in existing dense settlements was another factor. Thornhill was largely dependent on borehole water pumped into reservoirs and reticulated to public stand-pipes.[17] In 1995 the pumps were not operating fully and some piping had been damaged: people plumbed-in their own illegal taps resulting in higher leakage and lack of water in standpipes downstream. One small way in which pensions were redistributed was the payment by some old people to youths who fetched them water.

In moving to unoccupied land, some of the settlers clearly perceived that there might be agricultural potential, especially for livestock. But the majority of families, as often noted in the literature on black rural areas in South Africa, had very limited dependence on agriculture for their income. A survey which included questions on income generation showed about 40 per cent of families had a few livestock or ran chickens but—except for a small number of wealthier families—the income from this source was small compared to migrant wages and state welfare payments. In Thornhill about one quarter of the adult women, mostly under 30, and nearly half of the men, were recorded as absent at work; few worked locally. About one-fifth of people had pensions or disability grants.[18] Pensions and other welfare payments as well as income from the informal sector were especially important for the poorest families, almost by definition those without access to wages. Erosion of agricultural activity amongst poor families is hardly unique to South Africa. Dependence on wages earned at a distance, or welfare payments, gives families a certain mobility within range of the pension source. It is another factor in helping to understand why people are prepared to move into new informal settlements, and to do so in such numbers that access to agricultural land becomes very constrained.

A further element in mobility is youth: a disproportionate number of younger people settled in RA 60. It was more difficult for them to find sites in established villages, where they would probably have to pay headmen for land. Although a number of settlers, especially in Tambo village, were from towns and farms some distance away, there is evidence that local families adopted a strategy of multiple settlement. They might keep one site in Sada or Thornhill, where schools were better, while younger members of the family moved to Tambo village or Merino Walk. This was a sensible strategy. Not only did it ensure a residential site nearby with a garden for younger members of the family, but free land was likely to acquire some value.

Some Consequences of the Spread of Dense Settlement

There are clearly benefits for poor families in gaining access to these resources. In many ways this invasion was an exciting development. State land, which was effectively unoccupied, largely hired out to commercial ranchers, was taken over by an organized movement of the rural poor. Their action caught the attention of NGOs and government and the area was prioritized for further land acquisition and investment.

But there were also costs. Parts of the white-owned rural areas of South Africa, such as Queenstown district, had been the site of intensive agricultural investment in the shape of fences, dams, boreholes, and irrigation for over a century. For example, the fencing on a large pastoral farm sometimes represented three or four generations of investment and it is prohibitively expensive to begin from scratch. Fencing is essential for more sophisticated systems of pasture rotation long advocated by both farmers and the state. Arable farming and especially irrigated vegetables also require fencing unless animals are very carefully herded.

Where farms were taken into homelands, such as in the northern Ciskei since the 1970s, fences were often damaged. A number of different, if related, factors led to defencing. Probably most important in the areas around RA 60 was the requirement for fencing material itself. Fencing is expensive and large amounts of wire, posts, and gates stood with only limited protection around the countryside. Families moving into the dense settlements needed some privacy from pigs, hens, goats, and trespassers. Fences were also a means of defining boundaries in a situation where claims were not easily subject to legal enforcement and rights to land were fluid. The need to control space made fencing around a homestead and garden site a valuable asset. Fencing material formerly used for farm grazing paddocks or camps was recycled for use around residential and garden plots in dense settlements—or for small animal kraals. Most of the appropriation of fencing seems to have been done by individuals, but there was a small trade in stolen fencing materials.

Fencing was initially laid out for commercial farms and it is now not always appropriately placed. Settlements established near fenced roads, for example, may not have sufficient gates to offer easy access. If routes developing in the new social geography of the dense settlements, for example between villages or to schools, cut across fences, then the barrier disappeared. Public footpaths and direct routes are important for people who have to walk. Fences can also suffer if they stand in the way of the shortest routes to pasturage. Animals were often brought back to the homestead site at night in order to diminish the risk of theft and straying.

On the boundaries between African settlements and state, municipal, or private farm land, the erosion of fencing can be a more political process. Fences were being cut in the mid-1990s in order to harass farm owners. In some cases such action was directly related to a land claim. But even if this was not the case, both communities and farmers were well aware that such pressure might help to persuade white farmers to give up and sell out.[19] Cutting of fences is not necessarily systematic: for example, stock owners from communal areas might be attracted to the richer pastures in a rested farm grazing camp and, exploiting fence holes, put their animals there for a very limited time. Once fences are breached, boundaries become more permeable and stock stray.

White farmers around RA 60 were convinced that their capacity to protect their boundaries was diminishing. Aside from fence-cutting, theft, fire, and dogs were perceived as major problems. A few farmers in this area ceased trying to repair fences because it was too expensive. Instead, in an echo of the nineteenth century, before fences became universal on the commercial farms, they resorted to impounding stock. They transported stray livestock to Queenstown rather than Whittlesea because it was further away and more expensive for owners to liberate their animals.[20] Most of the farms around RA 60 were for sale. Even those farmers who felt that they could cope with the immediate pressures were concerned that their neighbours might sell and that prices would go down. In their perception, this area immediately south of Queenstown, the narrow northern neck of the old Border corridor, was going to become increasingly difficult as a site for commercial farming, whether for white or black owners.

The mobility of people and fences must be set next to changing patterns of stock-keeping, especially the rise of the goat. In the former Ciskei and on the western peripheries of the former Transkei, goat numbers seem to have increased relative to cattle and especially sheep. No general recent figures were available but the area was clearly heavily stocked.[21] Goats were both symptomatic of the state of agriculture and contributed to the impact of dense settlement. People tended to use two main explanations for the increase in the number of goats: drought and custom. First and perhaps most important, goats were perceived to be, and under the prevailing conditions almost certainly were, more capable of withstanding drought and limited grazing resources. Except immediately around dense settlements, much of the area had a good cover of *Acacia karoo*, a good browsing plant for goats but less attractive to sheep. Acacia may have spread over the longer term.[22] Goats and cattle were also perceived to be more difficult targets for both predators and theft. Sheep were especially vulnerable to jackals, caracals, and dogs. Stock theft was prevalent although fear of it was sometimes used as a metaphor by both white and black livestock owners for general lack of control and anxiety about property. Goats were also seen to be more suitable for customary slaughters.

The value of even a few head of stock to poor families should not be underestimated. Sale of a goat could then fetch around one third of the monthly pension. Along with pigs and chickens, they provided a means by which poor rural people could realize something from the communal pasture-land to which they had access. Goats, good colonizers, are generally more adept at fending for themselves in the semi-arid and semi-fenced pastures where animals are not always carefully herded. The type of stock kept does not of course in itself shape property relations but, in this context, where fences and tight demarcations of property were fraying, goats were in the vanguard of counter-colonization.

The decline of cultivation on African smallholdings in this area meant that there was less urgency to control goats; conversely, their prevalence was one factor which discouraged arable or even vegetable farming. Fields had not been demarcated in RA 60 seven years after its occupation. Some people tried to grow vegetables and peaches in gardens adjacent to their houses but this was greatly constrained by insecure fencing, inadequate water, and high mobility. (Cultivation was more widespread in parts of the Transkei and Ciskei where rainfall is higher, animals more systematically controlled, and where homesteads are closer to fields.)

Agricultural officials, farmers, and conservationists in the Eastern Cape see free-range livestock and the decline of fencing both as symptom and cause of agrarian problems. But range ecologists have questioned the wisdom of tight rotational systems in African contexts and explored the effectiveness of local regulation of commonages.[23] In this view, the loss of fences is not necessarily of great importance. They may have been appropriate to a system of stock-keeping pursued by large, and formerly subsidized, private land-owners—but alternative systems are not necessarily less efficient or more damaging. Some argue that heavy continuous grazing may not be highly selective or permanently alter the veld.[24] The dynamic of pastoral activities in common property systems calls for a different logic and more flexible prescriptions.[25] Such views are clearly attractive in a context where significant additional land is likely to come under some form of common or trust ownership. After years of heavy-handed intervention in the rural areas, it would certainly be difficult and politically unwise for the state to attempt any ambitious regulation that cuts directly across the patterns emerging on the ground. However, the costs of decapitalization should not be ignored. The development of dispersed dense settlements, where plot holders have small gardens, surrounded by relatively open-access pastureland might facilitate heavy stocking but it severely constrains agricultural investment of most kinds. In RA 60, self-settled by poor families, agriculture was certainly very difficult. Nor was there enough grazing land for more than a small proportion of the 2,000 households then estimated in the area, to own significant numbers of stock. Even if the carrying capacity was underestimated by officials at 6 ha. per large stock unit, this effectively meant there was enough land for an average of less than one head of cattle or a few goats per household.

We certainly need more research on pasture quality and sustainability under different property regimes in particular parts of South Africa. While it is clearly essential to work with communities, some of the ideas put forward in the new range ecology may have better application to areas of lower population density where labour is available for herding and local political authority more secure. There was certainly visual evidence of environmental problems around the dense settlements and the potential for rapid environmental degradation through unregulated heavy stocking in these areas.

Some Implications for Land Reform

The occupation of RA 60 was part of a significant rural popular movement, organized by politicized communities challenging the last remnants of the apartheid and homeland governments. A number of poor rural families were able to gain access to residential land on reasonably big garden plots—and also some access to communal grazing land. But it presented problems for any land reform planning in which agriculture was to play a major part.

Over the next couple of years, the momentum of land invasions of the type described on RA 60 was not maintained in the area around Queenstown. There was continued movement onto state and municipally-owned land around many of the small and medium-size towns in the Eastern Cape: each came to have its informal shack settlement. There were occasional incursions onto land privately owned by whites, and there was a good deal of harassment of commercial farmers, including fence cutting, and veld burning. The Eastern Cape was not exempt from the spate of murders of white farmers at this time. One of these incidents of temporary incursion onto white-owned land in 1993 was important in persuading the owner of Gallawater farm, adjacent to the Zweledinga settlement, to sell in 1995. But there were not many sustained attempts to take over farmland still occupied by private owners.

Thus the occupation of RA 60 was something of a special case—at least in respect of its scale. Yet the patterns of settlement established there to some degree replicated those in adjacent areas of the Ciskei and it seemed important to comprehend the dynamics which produced them. Clearly, land was the object of local political competition, as well as an asset for poor families. Evidently it was difficult for the state or communities to control the number of people moving on to free land. And in the political context of post-1994 South Africa, once people had moved onto new land, whatever the tenure conditions, it would be difficult and undesirable to move them off again. In fact the state has been cautious on this front and there have been few forced removals.

During discussions with communities moving on to new land, it was also clear that many people prioritized residential land and services rather than agricultural land—water, electricity, clinics, schools, and retail outlets. That was one reason why they clustered together in large villages on newly occupied land. At meetings about a farm purchase which we attended, for example, the community was concerned that enough people should move to qualify for a state-aided primary school, despite the fact that this would mean a density of settlement which would imply average stock-holdings of about 1.5 large stock units per family. Researchers detected a division between, on the one hand, women and younger people who prioritized services and preferred denser settlements and, on the other, older men, especially stock-owners, who were more concerned about having access to pasture. Dispersed dense settlement might be seen as a compromise between contending needs and priorities within households and communities.

Thus the problem of acquiring and allocating land was one of the most difficult procedures in thinking about the early phases of land reform—at least if agricultural production was to be maintained. There were tens of thousands of poor families in the area: who should benefit and how could a rush onto new land be avoided? The Department of Land Affairs was initially more concerned about the political dimensions of land redistribution, and less so about the issues of production. In radical land lobbies, there was a belief that smallholders on communally owned land would be able, with time and assistance, to organize themselves for agricultural production.[26] But the state responded to this dilemma partly by reluctance to purchase land directly and then decide on its allocation. If the Department acquired land in politically sensitive areas that were of key importance for land reform, it would have been difficult to control occupation, to adjudicate between claims or to place limits on the number of people moving.

The alternative that was pursued was for state agencies and NGOs to broker and subsidize purchases by self-organized trusts with a limited number of members so that ownership passed directly to these groups. Similar trust purchases had a long history in South Africa and this was the system provided for under Act 126 of 1993 (Certain Lands for Settlement) passed by the previous government, as a means by which African land acquisition could be facilitated outside of the homelands. Although they were expensive to establish and depended on subsidized legal services, trusts members would in theory have an interest in regulating entry. Small trusts, one for each farm purchased, also promised to inhibit the expansion of Tribal Authorities which still effectively controlled customary tenure in former homeland areas. The BRC itself was strongly opposed to facilitating the effective extension of chieftaincies. The idea of 'community', which has been ubiquitous in government and NGO circles, did not include 'traditional' communities in this sense, and most agencies working around the pilot schemes agreed with this approach. The proposed vehicle for land acquisition was thus a form of private tenure, but with multiple trust members, who would all have access to the land acquired.

The question arose as to whether there was any place for individual small or medium holders in the pilot schemes. This approach was strongly advocated in reports and proposals on land reform in South Africa funded by the World Bank in the early 1990s and also by the Liptons in the earlier phases of a large research programme which they co-ordinated.[27] It was initially proposed in the Free State land reform pilot. The state scheme envisaged for RA 60 prior to the invasion in 1991 included privately-held individual farming units of about 200 hectares, so that their owners could in theory derive a significant portion of their income from agriculture.

The idea was not entirely ruled out in the pilot scheme although it presented particular problems in selecting beneficiaries: could the state be seen to select and subsidize individuals on private farms of this size? Some commentators argued that privately held farms were more likely to be packed with tenants than land held by communities and trusts; it is true that, historically, many small farms privately held by black owners in the Eastern Cape have been heavily tenanted. Individual allocations were also politically difficult. When the invasion of RA 60 took place in 1991, some 1,600 ha. to the east of the main tarred road was not settled. This area had been fenced into small farms of about 150–200 ha., including irrigable land along the Klipplaat river. A number of meetings were held in 1994 and 1995 in order to discuss their allocation. Although Land Affairs officials continued to push the idea of privately held farms, representatives from RA 60 communities consistently argued that this land should be made available to them. They suggested strongly that they would make it very difficult for individual farmers to establish themselves; Murray charted a similar outcome in the Free State where one Botsabelo community group threatened to *toyi-toyi* any substantial individual beneficiary off the land.[28] This 1,600 ha. area adjacent to RA 60 was not allocated to individual farmers and eventually became an extension of community grazing land.

More general evidence on agricultural initiatives on communally occupied, or trust-purchased farms in the Eastern Cape in the 1990s was mixed. A largely self-organized irrigation scheme was developed on land occupied by farm workers in the Stockenstrom district of the former Ciskei. This was a former white-owned farm bought by the Ciskei government in the 1980s with its irrigation equipment and left rather moribund until taken over by the farmworkers, some of whom had stayed on the land.[29] Some of those who occupied Merino Walk in RA 60 purchased two adjacent farms with state assistance and, despite considerable difficulties, initiated vegetable production as well as running cattle and goats.[30]

However, the Zweledinga Residents Association, who purchased Gallawater farm, experienced considerable problems of investment, environmental management, and production.[31] One hundred and two people, about 10 per cent women, contributed to purchase the c.1,000 ha. farm, with a state subsidy of about 80 per cent. A complex trust, negotiated at length with the purchasers, established a framework for ownership and management; nine community leaders were chosen as trustees. They took occupation, amidst national news coverage, in 1995 and about 30 trust members had moved onto the farm by October 1997.

The method of purchase by a trust does seem to have been effective, at least in the short term, in limiting numbers on the farm. But a number of interrelated problems arose over the next two years. The infrastructure on the farm deteriorated. Fences between Gallawater and its neighbours were not kept up, resulting in animals straying and heavy expenditure on pound fees. The irrigation furrow supplying 34 ha. of irrigable land became blocked. Electricity and telephone bills were not paid so that these services were cut off and the pump from the Klipplaat river, which supplied household taps, and dispersed stock troughs, could not function. Women had to collect water from the river and stock were brought to the river to drink, which was not only leading to denudation on its banks but exposing the arable fields to damage. Only a few patches of dryland maize had been planted.

These problems arose not simply because those settled on the farm were poor; the trust included a number of substantial stock-owners. A survey recorded 275 cattle, 238 sheep, and 340 goats on the farm. Animals were frequently sold off the farm. However, most of the stock on the farm belonged to relatively few owners and most of these were not resident on the farm. They used their trust membership to extend their access to grazing but did not put their profits back into the trust. Financial mechanisms providing for this could not be enforced and an attempt to collect a grazing levy was unsuccessful. Gallawater should have received more state support after the purchase, given that it was a pioneering land transfer in the area. But developments on Gallawater suggested that this form of trust ownership also required careful reconsideration. Poorer families on the farm clearly did receive some benefit in access to land, grazing, and firewood (the river valley has a dense acacia cover). And there was clearly potential for development. But up to 1997, a few absent trust members benefited disproportionately, and investment was minimal.

My experience of these complex social dynamics—analysed only in outline here—around land in the area of the pilot land reform scheme led me to modify my views about appropriate strategies for agricultural land reform. Clearly there was an overwhelming need to provide poor people with adequate and secure residential land, on plots that were as large as possible, so that they were able to build dwellings and develop gardens. The size of plots in the pilot areas, around a quarter of a hectare, were larger than those in most urban areas. Servicing such new settlements with water and electricity was also urgent. But it made more sense for essentially residential developments such as those on RA 60, and others that were taking shape, to be located around existing conurbations. The potential for smallholder agriculture on such land did not look promising, although it may be a couple of decades before the long-term possibilities become clear. The state and its agencies could not fully control the process of occupation and land reform. Some involved in NGOs and community land groups in the Eastern Cape in the 1990s preferred a more customary or communalist approach even if this did mean denser settlement. These forms of tenure still dominated in the former homelands and provided some resources for poorer families, not least for women. It may be that in the medium term, farms owned by more restrictive trusts will be effectively communalized, as on RA 60. This may yet become the most common form of occupation on land adjacent to the former homelands in the Border corridor. This form of dense settlement or communally owned trust farms has spread in South Africa.[32] Such outcomes were also the result of legal land restitution process. It seemed to me that policy in pursuit of land reform that prioritized agriculture should avoid communal forms of tenure, and explore ways of limiting the number of people settling on newly acquired land. Fast track land reform in Zimbabwe after 2000 has also resulted in declining production—at least in the short term.

The ANC government did in fact shift its policies. There were many factors involved, including concerns about food security, a general reorientation towards growth rather than redistribution, pressure from African farmers' associations and from organized commercial farmers. The pilot land reform schemes were not fully implemented and were effectively abandoned by the late 1990s. In the Eastern Cape, the Department of Land Affairs continued to facilitate land purchases by groups using the R15,000 individual state subsidies (gradually increased) together with other grants. Private individual purchases by black owners probably become the most important element in land transfers by the late 1990s. Not least because of the problems outlined above, local Land Affairs officials took an increasingly cautious approach to land acquisition by trusts that included large numbers of members.

In 1999, under a new Minister, the Departments of Land Affairs and Agriculture began to articulate a new emphasis on individual 'emerging farmers'. There have been many attempts to speed up the process, but the state has not prioritized land reform, and budgets have been limited. So has the administrative capacity. The question remains whether this gradualist approach, which has so far enabled agricultural production to be sustained, will be an adequate political response—or whether populist politicians, and popular rural movements, following the Zimbabwean example, choose to mobilize more radically around the land issue. The two poles of power in the South African countryside in the apartheid era were white-controlled commercial agriculture and chiefs or tribal authorities in command of rural districts under customary or communal forms of tenure. Agricultural production has survived in some of the latter areas, but seldom thrived. Neither of these agrarian systems provided much scope for African medium-holders—men or women ambitious to invest in agriculture. Nor did the communalist orientation of the early attempts at land reform. The ANC now appears to be searching for some middle ground.

Endnotes

Notes to Chapter 1

1. Quoted by Anne Barron, 'No Other Law? Author-ity, Property and Aboriginal Art', in Lionel Bently and S. Mariatis (eds), *Intellectual Property and Ethics* (London: Sweet and Maxwell, 1998), p. 54; the date is 1971. It seemed to the court that people were claiming to relate to land either as members of a territorial band or as members of a clan that has its sacred imprint on the landscape. The judge could also have been drawing inspiration from the Torrens system of land registration in Australia, by which title relates not to an owner's various holdings but to a holding's various owners (see Annelise Riles, 'Law as Object', in Sally Merry and Donald Brenneis (eds), *Law and Empire in the Pacific: Fiji and Hawai'i* (Santa FeC School of American Research Press, 2003)).
2. Daniel de Coppet, 'Land Owns People . . . ', in Robert Barnes, Daniel de Coppet and Robert Parkin (eds), *Contexts and Level: Anthropological Essays on Hierarchy* (Oxford: Journal of the Anthropological Society of Oxford, Occasional Papers, 1985).
3. This was given to Daniel de Coppet by the late Aliki Nono'ohimae Eerehau; ibid., p. 81.
4. Gisa Weskalnys, *Alexanderplatz: An Ethnographic Study of Place and Planning in Contemporary Berlin*, Ph.D. dissertation (Cambridge University), 130. I am most grateful for permission to quote from this unpublished dissertation.
5. She quotes one woman who was very clear that this was not a matter of attachment term to external, material things, for identity had to be found within: she enfolded within her memories of Alexanderplatz in earlier times.

6. Weskalnys calls this 'societal property' (ibid., p. 129), 'societal' being more satisfactory than 'illusory' that Rose uses: illusory property 'involves the imaginative construction of property even where the law recognizes none' (Carol Rose, *Property and Persuasion: Essays in the History, Theory and Rhetoric of Ownership* (Boulder, Co.: Westview Press, 1994), 274).
7. Known as Incorporated Land Groups (ILCs). Anthropological discussions include Thomas Ernst, 'Land, Stories and Resources: Discourse and Entification in Onabasulu Modernity', *American Anthropologist* 101 (1999), 88–97; Colin Filer, 'The Role of Landowning Communities in PNG's Mineral Policy Framework', in W. Bastida, T. Wälde, and J. Warden (eds), *International and Comparative Mineral Law and Policy* (The Hague: Kluwer International, 2003); Eric Hirsch, 'New Boundaries of Influence in Highland Papua: "Culture", Mining and Ritual Conversions', *Oceania* 71 (2001), 293–1; James Weiner, 'The Foi Incorporated Land Group: Law and Custom in Group Definition and Collective Action in the Kutubu Oil Project Area', paper given to PTC Colloquium, Cambridge 2000, n.d. Ian Marru's unpublished M.Phil. thesis (Cambridge University, 2004) is on ILCs.
8. See, for example, Tony Crook, 'Transactions in Perpetual Motion', in Eric Hirsch and Marilyn Strathern (eds), *Transactions and Creations: Property Debates and the Stimulus of Melanesia* (Oxford: Berghahn, 2004); Lawrence Kalinoe, 'Compensating Alienated Customary Land in Papua New Guinea: Rethinking its Rationale and its Regime', Macmillan Brown Working Paper series, 10 (Christchurch: University of Canterbury, 2004); Stuart Kirsch, 'Lost Worlds: Environmental Disaster, "Culture Loss" and the Law', *Current Anthropology*, 42 (2001), 67–98.
9. Only about 3% of the land is not under customary tenure; 85% of the population are 'subsistence farmers', in the main horticulturalists and thus known in the literature as gardeners. Some of the issues this poses to mineral development are laid out in the consultation paper of the Papua New Guinea Department

of Petroleum and Energy, *Regulation of Social Mapping and Landowner Identification* (Port Moresby, 2002), with thanks to John Rivers.

10. I generalize, of course, across myriad local diversities, and my remarks refer to men more than to women.
11. De Coppet, 'Land Owns People . . . ', 84 expresses his surprise at the switch in Aliki Nono'ohimae Eerehaua's text.
12. I draw directly here from James Leach's work, especially his book *Creative Land: Place and Procreation on the Rai Coast of Papua New Guinea* (Oxford: Berghahn Books, 2003), as well as 'Land, Trees and History' in Lawrence Kalinoe and James Leach (eds), *Rationales of Ownership: Transactions and Claims to Ownership in Contemporary Papua New Guinea* (Wantage: Sean Kingston Publishing, 2004). More generally, see Hirsch and Strathern (eds), *Transactions and Creations*; Eric Hirsch, 'Environment and Economy: Mutual Connections and Diverse Perspectives', *Anthropological Theory*, 4 (2004), 435–53.
13. Sherman and Bently find this more widely articulated in the past than in the present, where many claim that contemporary British intellectual property law, with its pragmatic and positive heritage, is not on the face of it concerned with creativity but rather with the expenditure of effort by which people create, i.e. make, things in a very limited sense (Brad Sherman and Lionel Bently, *The Making of Modern Intellectual Property Law: the British Experience, 1760–1911* (Cambridge: Cambridge University Press, 1999).
14. A point made by Anne Barron, 'No Other Law?'.
15. Tony Crook in 'Transactions' alludes to the way in which a group in (what it regarded as) the vicinity of the mine presented its petition for damages. In their eyes, a description of the state of their land and rivers would be enough to make their case.
16. After Eric Hirsch, 'Boundaries of Creation: The Work of Credibility in Science and ceremony', in Hirsch and Strathern (eds), *Transactions and Creations*. Obviously this foray into legal matters

is a limited exercise on my part. For reflections that convey some of the complexity of legal concerns with property, see Kevin Gray, 'Equitable Property', in M. D. A. Freeman with R. Halson (eds), *Current Legal Problems 1994, Part 2: Collected Papers* (Oxford: Oxford University Press, 1994); Kevin Gray and Susan Gray, 'The Idea of Property in Land', in Susan Bright and John Dewar (eds), *Land Law: Themes and Perspectives* (Oxford: Oxford University Press, 1998).

17. Principally to the extent to which it is useful at all to borrow the term 'property'. See n. 19.
18. World Intellectual Property Organization (WIPO), Trade-Related Aspects of Intellectual Property Rights agreement (TRIPS).
19. The right to own property is recognized in the UN Universal Declaration on Human Rights and the International Convention on the Elimination of All Forms of Racial Discrimination as a fundamental human right that extends to everyone; see for example T. Simpson, *Indigenous Heritage and Self-determination: the Cultural and Intellectual Property Rights of Indigenous People* (Copenhagen: IWGIA, International Work Group for indigenous Affairs, 1997). Simpson observes that such international legal instruments 'do not draw on the principles of indigenous customary law'; rather, they 'assume that the sovereignty of the National State and the concept of exclusive possession lie at the heart of property rights, thereby denying the existence of collective ownership and the non-transferability of ownership, which are central to indigenous property systems', p. 65. The UN mounted a strong criticism that the IPR regime embodied in the TRIPS agreement of 1994 was at odds with international human rights law (paraphrase from the UN Sub-Committee on the Promotion and Protection of Human Rights, 2000). It called for the World Treaty Organization (WTO) to take into account existing state regulations under international human rights law.

20. Alberto Corsín Jiménez, 'On Space as a Capacity', *Journal of the Royal Anthropological Institute* (NS) 9 (2003), 137–53 at p. 146.
21. What follows is my extrapolation, not a conversation as I have presented it here.
22. Trees have appeared in all kinds of anthropological accounts, notably Laura Rival (ed)'s, *The Social Life of Trees: Anthropological Perspectives on Tree Symbolism* (Oxford: Berg, 1998), esp. the chapter by Maurice Bloch, 'Why Trees, too, are Good to Think with: Towards an Anthropology of the Meaning of Life'.
23. More than an anthropological observation, this is built into policy presumptions in Papua New Guinea. See Department of Petroleum, *Regulation of Social Mapping*; Lawrence Kalinoe, 'Legal Options for the Regulation of Intellectual and Cultural Property in Papua New Guinea', in Hirsch and Strathern (eds), *Transactions and Creations*, 41–2.
24. Among many points not separately acknowledged that arose in the discussion at LSE (see Acknowledgements).
25. See Rosemary Coombe, *The Cultural Life of Intellectual Properties: Authorship, Appropriation and the Law* (Durham, NC: Duke University Press, 1998).
26. As laid out in the textbook by David Bainbridge, *Intellectual Property*, 4th ed. (London: Financial Times Management & Pitman Publishing, 1999).
27. Roy Wagner explores the phenomenology of this in 'The Fractal Person', in Maurice Godelier and Marilyn Strathern (eds), *Big Men and Great Men: Personifications of Power in Melanesia* (Cambridge: Cambridge University Press, 1991).
28. The classic statement about 'kinds' is to be found in Rita Astuti, *People of the Sea: Identity and Descent among the Vezo of Madagascar* (Cambridge: Cambridge University Press, 1995).
29. From Mark Rose, *Authors and Owners: the Invention of Copyright* (Cambridge, MA: Harvard University Press, 1993), 41, 58. Whether or not copyright can be considered property is sometimes questioned; this is partly because of its unusual legal status

(it exists not in fact but only in law; it can be infringed but not 'stolen', and rather than being a thing protected for as long as it exists suddenly ceases to exist at the end of a set term), but partly because 'a sizeable body of otherwise intelligent persons . . . argue from the mistaken premise that something cannot be truly "property" unless it is solid and has the attributes of a physical presence' (Jeremy Phillips and Alison Firth, *Introduction to Intellectual Property Law* (2nd ed.) (London: Butterworths,1990), 107.

30. Rose, *Authors and Owners*, 40.
31. According to Rose; ibid. 38.
32. Widely documented in Melanesia; for a case from Papua New Guinea, see Hirsch 'New Boundaries of Influence'.
33. This is a major theme to emerge from the work of Nancy Munn on Gawa Island, part of the extensive archipelago that lies off the south east coast of Papua New Guinea, see n. 34.
34. Nancy Munn, *The Fame of Gawa: A Symbolic Study of Value Transformation in a Massim (Papua New Guinea) Society* (Cambridge: Cambridge University Press, 1986).
35. In reference to the clan body, she smears the tree with her body fluids. Through matrilineal subclans, women are the originating source of land-based raw materials such as wood; ibid. 140.
36. The people of Goodenough Island, in the same island chain, recount the pathetic story (myth) of the man who, wanting to wear it himself, coveted a pendant that was actually part of the living flesh of his wife; cutting it from her, he killed her and was in turn killed (Michael Young, 'The tusk, the flue and the serpent: disguise and revelation in Goodenough mythology', in Marilyn Strathern (ed.), *Analysing Gender Relations in Melanesia and Beyond* (Cambridge: Cambridge University Press, 1977), 241–3).
37. Eerehau (de Coppet, 'Land Owns People', 84–5) said that when it comes to people owning land, one of the indications is that the person's *tree* is there. One's 'tree', especially for a man, means all one's achievements, assistance rendered to others, wealth

disbursed: 'success is seen as a superb tree rising high over [one's] land and embellishing it', with its roots in the soil and its lateral spread like 'a living transposition of an apical ancestor's extension after death', that is, the population that followed.

38. Documented, and elsewhere, in Leach's *Creative Land*.
39. Their matrilineal practices were made famous by Bronislaw Malinowski, and later by Annette Weiner.
40. I draw on Battaglia's study (Debbora Battaglia, 'Retaining Reality: Some Practical Problems with Objects as Property', *Man* (NS) 29: 3 (1994) 631–44; 'On Practical Nostalgia: Self-Prospecting among Urban Trobrianders', in Debbora Battaglia (ed.), *Rhetorics of Self-making* (Berkeley, CA: University of California Press, 1995).
41. This account is from Battaglia, 'Practical Nostalgia'.
42. Yams for display are those destined for the gardener's matrilineal kinswomen: he grows yam-children for his married sister(s). Other, smaller, yams help feed his wife's child.
43. Being able to complete the building of the cone in one go is a mark of aesthetic power.
44. For each measuring basket, a leaflet is torn from a large cycas frond, every tenth leaflet having only its tip taken, so a glance shows how many units have been measured out.
45. Bronislaw Malinowski, *Coral Gardens and their Magic* (New York: American Book Company, 1935), 177, 213 and Appendix (Document II).
46. Battaglia, 'Practical Nostalgia', 85.
47. The criticism was diminishing of people's efforts. When Trobriand men grow yams to give away, it accomplishes an aesthetic and political supplementation: 'A man is *more* for gardening—experiences more *of* himself and his relational capacity' (Battaglia, 'Practical Nostalgia', 80, original emphasis).
48. Trobrianders are said to value the intangible evidence of their creativity, horticultural, and social, over the satsifaction of

consumption. So people would rather have full gardens and empty stomachs than the other way round, just as instead of full stomachs after a harvest they would rather have full yam houses. On the critical management of display in another context, see Karen Sykes, 'Negotiating Interests in Culture', in Hirsch and Strathern (eds), *Transactions and Creations*.

49. Over and again the ethnographic record describes Melanesians making 'bodies' of persons that are also the bodies of groups by putting together the land's creations—food, wild plants, wealth, and so forth—sometimes as literal assemblages of such items, sometimes in stylised carved form or sculptures.
50. Again, well beyond anthropological analysis, the concept of 'compensation' has become a ubiquitous and often urgent policy matter. It was the Papua New Guinea Law Reform Commission that published *Compensation for Resource Development in Papua New Guinea*, ed. by Susan Toft (along with The Australian National University, 1997). Compensation payments for land spoilage are likely to far outweigh landowners' entitlement to royalties (where these have been negotiated); for a case in point see Burton, in Toft's volume.
51. From the chapters by Susanne Bonnell and John Burton, ibid. On the contentious use of the term 'landowner' see Colin Filer's contribution to the same volume.
52. From Lawrence Kalinoe, 'The Ok Tedi Community Mine Continuation Agreements: A Case Study in Dealing with Customary Landowners' Compensation Claims in Papua New Guinea', Port Moresby: School of Law, University of Papua New Guinea, 2004 (I am grateful for permission to cite this unpublished paper). Some background is given in Stuart Kirsch, 'Indigenous Response to Environmental Impact along the Ok Tedi', in Toft (ed.). *Compensation for Resource Development*; David Hyndman, 'Ok Tedi: New Guinea's Disaster Mine', *The Ecologist*, 18: 1 (1998), 24–9. On the Community Mine Continuation Agreements, see also Stuart Kirsch, 'Property

Limits: Debates on the Body, nature and culture', in Hirsch and Strathern (eds), *Transactions and Creations*, and Tony Crook ('Transactions' in *Transactions and Creations*).

53. Kalinoe, 'Compensating Alienated Customary Land'.
54. The clarity of the distinction has been overtaken by developments in biotechnology, as well as the communication technologies, e.g. Alain Pottage, 'The Inscription of Life in Law: genes, parents, and bio-politics', *Modern Law Review*, 61 (1998), 740–65.
55. A classic example of such play is found in Roy Wagner, 'Figure-ground Reversal among the Barok', in Louise Lincoln (ed.), *Assemblage of Spirits: Idea and Image in New Ireland* (New York: George Braziller, in assoc. the Minneapolis Institute of Arts, 1987). The trick of making things visible is to find the form in which they are to appear; see Melissa Demian's comments on property in this context, 'Seeing, Knowing, Owning: Property Claims as Revelatory Acts', in Hirsch and Strathern (eds), *Transactions and Creations*.
56. With profound acknowledgement to Darrell Posey and his work on traditional resource rights at the Oxford Centre for Environment, Ethics, and Society, Mansfield College. Much of the material here comes from work undertaken for an ESRC funded project 'Property, Transactions, Creations: New Economic Relations in the Pacific' (PTC) (with acknowledgement of research award no. R000237838), and colleagues on that project will recognise their ideas here. The Anthropology Seminar at the London School of Economics gave this lecture shape.

Notes to Response to Chapter 1

1. See also M. Strathern and E. Hirsch, 'Introduction' in M. Strathern and E. Hirsch (eds), *Transactions and Creations: Property Debates and the Stimulus of Melanesia* (Oxford: Berghahn Books, 2004), 1–19.

2. With the added consequence, judiciously noted by Kirsch, that we assume property rights to be held by individuals in Euro-America, but collectively by indigenous peoples. See S. Kirsch, 'Property Limits: Debates on the Body, Nature and Culture' in Hirsch and Strathern, *Transactions and Creations*, 21–39.
3. M. Radin, *Contested Commodities* (Cambridge MA: Harvard University Press, 1996), 75–6.
4. That is, at once legal and moral. See M. Fortes, *Kinship and the Social Order: the Legacy of Lewis Henry Morgan* (London: Routledge, 1970).
5. E. Wolf, 'Ownership and Political Ecology', *Anthropology Quarterly* 45: 3 (1972), 201–5.
6. 'National Citizenship, Private Property, and Domestic Migration: Witches' Brew?', The Fifth Annual Harrell-Bond Lecture. Refugee Studies Centre, University of Oxford, 13th October 2004.
7. 'The Trouble with "Nature" and "Natural Resources" ', presented at the Queen Elizabeth House, Oxford, 50th Anniversary Conference, 2–5 July, 2005.
8. *Meeting the Universe Half Way: Quantum Physics and the Entanglement of Matter and Meaning* (Durham: Duke University Press, 2006).
9. See in particular M. Strathern 'Cutting the Network', *Journal of the Royal Anthropological Institute* 23 (1996), 517–35.
10. Strathern and Hirsch, *Transactions and Creations*, 5.
11. *The Anthropology of Economy: Community, Market, and Culture* (Oxford: Blackwell, 2001). Any economy, according to Gudeman, contains two domains: 'impersonal trade' or 'market' on the one hand, and 'mutuality' or 'community' on the other. These two realms of the economy are characterized by two different kinds of property ('commensurate property' or capital vs 'base' or shared holdings) and two different modes of distribution ('apportionment' vs 'allotment'). The base is a kind of heritage, which partly overlaps with the environment,

as it includes material resources, symbols, and landscapes. The base is 'a legacy, a making and a reservoir'.

Notes to Response to Chapter 2

1. http://www.iwgia.org/graphics/Synkron-Library/Documents/Noticeboard/News/International/DDadopted.htm
2. Ibid.
3. http://www.iwgia.org/graphics/Synkron-Library/Documents/Noticeboard/News/International/IPclosingstatementHRC2006.htm

Notes to Chapter 3

1. 21 US (1823) 240 at 253.
2. *In re Southern Rhodesia* [1919] AC 211 at 232.
3. Ibid. 233–4.
4. Ibid. 234.
5. Ibid. 235.
6. Justice Brennan (Mason CJ and McHugh J concurring) in *Mabo v Queensland (No. 2)* (1992) 175 CLR 1 at 41–2.
7. Ibid. 42.
8. The editorial of the *British Medical Journal* (Vol. 327: 404 (23 August 2003)) recently reported: 'The gap in life expectancy between indigenous and non-indigenous populations is estimated to be 19–21 years in Australia, 8 years in New Zealand, 5–7 years in Canada, and 4–5 years in the United States. These continuing disparities in health are a matter of major concern, but it is none the less important to recognise the substantial narrowing of the gap in health between indigenous and non-indigenous people in the United States, Canada, and New Zealand. In Australia the gap in median age at death seems to have widened.'
9. Professor Fiona Stanley, Australian of the Year in 2003, wrote in the *British Medical Journal* (ibid.) 'In Australia, there is currently a

debate about symbolic versus practical reconciliation—the latterapproach suggesting that it is best not to acknowledge the history and its influence on current outcomes, and that to move forward to improve living conditions and other activities that enhance wellbeing is in effect ignoring the root causes. However, evidence shows that the most effective programmes are those which acknowledge the devastating impact of removing people from their land, removing children from their families and from their culture, and marginalising people so that they cannot access any of the advantages of the dominant culture, such as education and employment, which would have enabled them to participate and control their own lives.'

10. *Milirrpum* v *Nabalco* (1971) 17 FLR 141 at 267.
11. *Milirrpum* v *Nabalco*: (1971) 17 FLR 141 at 198.
12. *Mabo* v *Queensland* (1988) 166 CLR 186.
13. *Mabo* v *Queensland (No. 2)* (1992) 175 CLR 1 at 217.
14. That fund is now self-perpetuating, allowing purchases of $45 million each year. The indigenous Land Corporation has purchased 162 properties involving 5.1 million hectares at a cost of $136 million, of which 110 have been divested to indigenous corporations. The ILC estimates that 60,000 indigenous Australians derive some benefit from these purchases. However, only about 1,000 persons are receiving a direct, tangible benefit such as residence (474), full time employment (157) or part-time employment (383). While 68% of properties were occupied, only 30% of them were providing any employment.
15. *Native Title Act Case* (1995) 183 CLR 373, *North Ganalanja Aboriginal Corporation* v *Queensland* (1996) 185 CLR 595, *Wik Peoples* v *Queensland* (1996) 187 CLR 1, *Fejo* v *Northern Territory* (1998) 195 CLR 96, *Yanner* v *Eaton* (1999) 201 CLR 351, *Commonwealth* v *Yarmirr* (2001) 208 CLR 1, *Western Australia* v *Ward* (2002) 213 CLR 1, *Wilson* v *Anderson* (2002) 213 CLR 401, *Yorta Yorta* v *Victoria* (2002) 214 CLR 422. The key questions have been about the capacity of native title to co-exist with

other interests in land such as pastoral leases, and the relationship between common law native title and the native title rights defined in the Native Title Act 1994–8.

16. (1996) CPD (HofR) 345; 6 May 1996. Again on 26 June 1996, John Howard told Parliament: 'I have always regarded the *Mabo* decision itself as being a justified, correct decision. I have stated that on a number of occasions.' (1996) CPD (HofR) 2791.
17. Justices Deane and Gaudron, *Mabo* v *Queensland (No 2)* (1992) 175 CLR 1 at 104.
18. *Western Australia* v *Ward* (2002) 213 CLR 1 at 240–1. (This case deals with the claim by the Miriuwung and Gajerrong People to lands in the East Kimberley region of Western Australia, including part of the Ord River scheme.) During argument in the earlier case *Fejo* v *Northern Territory* (1998) 195 CLR 96, Justice McHugh said during argument: 'My view was that native title would apply basically to only unalienated Crown land. If, for example, I thought it was going to apply to freehold, to leaseholds, I am by no means convinced that I would have not joined Justice Dawson (the sole dissentient in *Mabo*), and it may well be that that was also the view of other members of the Court.' (Transcript 22 June 1998)
19. In *Wilson* v *Anderson* (2002) 213 CLR 401 at 454, Justice Kirby said: 'The legal advance that commenced with *Mabo* v *Queensland (No 2)* or perhaps earlier, has now attracted such difficulties that the benefits intended for Australia's indigenous peoples in relation to native title to land and waters are being channelled into costs of administration and litigation that leave everyone dissatisfied and many disappointed.'

    In *Western Australia* v *Ward* (2002) 213 CLR 1 at 398–9, Justice Callinan J said: 'I do not disparage the importance to the Aboriginal people of their native title rights, including those that have symbolic significance. I fear, however, that in many cases because of the chasm between the common law and native title rights, the latter, when recognised, will amount to little more than symbols.

It might have been better to redress the wrongs of dispossession by a true and unqualified settlement of lands or money than by an ultimately futile or unsatisfactory, in my respectful opinion, attempt to fold native title rights into the common law.'

20. N. Pearson, 'Where we've come from and where we're at with the opportunity that is Koiki Mabo's legacy to Australia', Mabo Lecture, AIATSIS Native Title Conference 2003, 'Native Title on the Ground', Alice Springs, 3–5 June 2003.
21. G. Neate, 'The "Tidal Wave" of Justice and the "Tide of History"', Address to 5th World Summit of Nobel Peace Laureates, Rome, 10 November 2004, 27.
22. J. Gobbo, 'Citizenship in Australia', Address to Australian Reconciliation Convention 1997.
23. J. Kerr, 'Reflections on the Northern Territory Cattle Station Industry Award Case of 1965 and the O'Shea case of 1969', Address to H R Nicholls Society, 28 February 1986.
24. *The Northern Territory Cattle Industry Case* (1965) 113 CAR 651 (Cth), followed up elsewhere in Australia in *Australian Workers Union* v *Graziers Association of New South Wales and Others* (1967) 121 CAR 454 (Cth).
25. 2004 CPD (HofR) 6; 29 November 2004.
26. The Australian Government has recently dismissed the elected Aboriginal and Torres Strait Islander Commission (ATSIC) and appointed its own National Indigenous Council. Senior indigenous leader Galarrwuy Yunupingu announced his withdrawal from public life at last year's Gama Festival saying he was 'sick of government making their own indigenous leaders'.
27. N. Pearson, 'A Fair Place In Our Own Country: Indigenous Australians, Land Rights And The Australian Economy', Castan Public Lecture, Castan Centre For Human Rights Law, Monash University, June 2004.
28. On 20 October 1974, Prime Minister Gough Whitlam wrote to Sir Joh Bjelke Petersen recalling their discussion in March 1974 about land rights. The Australian government 'did not

wish to push the matter ahead of the Aboriginal Land Rights Commission Report'. Now that the report had been received, every indication from the Queensland government was that the premier 'believed the whole question of Aboriginal land rights need no longer be discussed'. Stalling the matter, Sir Joh replied on 1 November 1974: 'It is a matter for you and your government to decide what action you propose to take. However, in the circumstances, it may be thought desirable to delay any possible action until further consultation has taken place between our respective ministers.'

29. Sir Joh Bjelke Petersen to Bishop W Murray, 8 February 1979.
30. J. Howard, *Lateline*, ABC Television, Australia, 28 September 2004.
31. *The Weekend Australian*, 4 December 2004.
32. Ibid.
33. P. Dodson, 'Why I've Changed my Mind', *The Australian*, 7 December 2004.
34. Letter to the Editor, *The Australian*, 18 January 2005.
35. Jack Snyder, 'One World, Rival Theories', in *Foreign Policy*, November/December 2004, 53 at p. 62.
36. Keith Windschuttle, *The Fabrication of Aboriginal History*, volume one, *Van Dieman's Land 1803–1847* (Sydney: Macleay Press, Melbourne 2002).
37. Stuart McIntyre, *The History Wars* (Melbourne: Melbourne University Press, 2003).
38. Stuart McIntyre (ed.), *The Historian's Conscience: Australian Historians on the Ethics of History* (Melbourne: Melbourne University Press, 2004.
39. Greg Dening 'Living with and in deep time', in McIntyre (ed.), *The Historian's Conscience*, 43.
40. T. Winton, 'Aquifer', in *The Turning* (Australia: Picador, 2004), 53.
41. 21 US (1823) 240 at 260. Marshall goes on to say: 'When the conquest is complete, and the conquered inhabitants can be blended with the conquerors, or safely governed as a distinct people, public opinion, which not even the conqueror can disregard, imposes

these restraints upon him; and he cannot neglect them, without injury to his fame, and hazard to his power.'

42. P. Keating, Australian Launch of the International Year for the World's Indigenous People, Redfern, 10 December 1992.
43. 2004 CPD (HofR) 6; 29 November 2004.

Notes to Response to Chapter 3

1. For a comparable argument derived from the indigenous experience in Canada see Wayne Warry, *Unfinished Dreams: Community-healing and the Reality of Aboriginal Self-Government* (Toronto: University of Toronto Press, 1998).
2. The Sub-Commission used to be known as the Sub-Commission on the Prevention of Discrimination and the Protection of Minorities.
3. Sarah Prichard (ed.), *Indigenous Peoples, the United Nations and Human Rights* (London and Leichhardt: Zed Books and the Federation Press, 1998).
4. Invitation letter from Harriet Cross of the Foreign and Commonwealth Office to NGOs to attend a meeting on indigenous rights, 23rd October 2002.
5. Fergus MacKay, The UN Draft Declaration on the Rights of Indigenous Peoples and the Position of the United Kingdom (Moreton-in-Marsh: Forest Peoples Programme, 2003).
6. For example, Angie Debo, 1940, *And Still the Waters Run: the Betrayal of the Five Civilized Tribes* (Princeton: Princeton University Press, 1940); Kent Carter, *The Dawes Commission and the Allotment of the Five Civilized Tribes 1893–1914* (Ancestry.com, 1999).
7. Marcus Colchester and Fergus Mackay, *In Search of Middle Ground: Indigenous Peoples, Collective Representation and the Right to Free, Prior and Informed Consent* (Moreton-in-Marsh: Forest Peoples Programme, 2004).

8. Tom Griffiths, 'Indigenous Peoples, Land Tenure and Land Policy in Latin America' in *Land Reform, Land Settlement and Cooperatives*, 1 (2004), 46–63.
9. For a useful discussion see Marie-Benedicte Dembour, 'Following the Movement of the Pendulum: between Universalism and Relativism' in Jane K. Cowan, Marie-Benedicte Dembour and Richard A. Wilson (eds.), *Culture and Rights: Anthropological Perspectives* (Cambridge: Cambridge University Press, 2004), 56–79.
10. Manila Declaration of the International Conference on Conflict Resolution, Peace Building, Sustainable Development and Indigenous Peoples, Metro Manila, Philippines, 6–8 December 2000.
11. Dan Russell, *A People's Dream: Aboriginal Self-Government in Canada* (Vancouver: University of British Columbia Press, 2000); Stephen L. Pevar, *The Rights of Indians and Tribes*, 2nd edition (Carbondale and Edwardsville: Southern Illinois University Press, 1992); see also Ellen Rose-Kambel, *A Guide to Indigenous Women's Rights under the International Convention on the Elimination of All Forms of Discrimination Against Women* (Moreton-in-Marsh: Forest Peoples Programme, 2004).

Notes to Response to Chapter 4

1. The River Niger flows from the north-west and the River Benue from the north-east; the Benue converges with the Niger at Lokoja, the capital city of Kogi State, situated to the south of the federal capital, Abuja.
2. Shell has various subsidiary companies in Nigeria, the largest being the Shell Petroleum and Development Company (SPDC).
3. For the full text see K. Saro-Wiwa, *Genocide in Nigeria: The Ogoni Tragedy* (London: Saros International Publishers, 1992). For further analysis see E. E. Osaghae, 'The Ogoni Uprising: Oil Politics, Minority Agitation and the Future of the Nigerian State', *African Affairs*, 94: 376 (July 1995), 325–44.

4. Ike Okonta and Oronto Douglas, *Where Vultures Feast: Shell, Human Rights, and Oil* (Verso: London and New York, 2003), 117.
5. K. Saro-Wiwa, *A Month and a Day: a Detention Diary* (London: Penguin, 1995).
6. Ibid.; see also Saro Wiwa, *Genocide in Nigeria*; Ken Wiwa, *In the Shadow of a Saint* (London: Black Swan, 2001).
7. Cited in Okonta and Douglas, *Where Vultures Feast*, 209.
8. Kathryn Nwajiaku, 'Between Discourse and Reality: The Politics of Oil and Ijaw Ethnic Nationalism in the Niger Delta', *Cahiers d'Études africaines*, 45: 2 (2005), 457–96 (p. 457).
9. Ibid.
10. Ibid. 458.
11. Ibid. 459.
12. I. Okonta, 'Behind the Mask: Explaining the Emergence of the MEND Militia in Nigeria's Oil-Bearing Niger Delta'. Institute of International Studies, University of California, Berkeley, 2006, pp. 11–12.
13. R. Blench, U. Hassan, and S. Longtau, 'The Impact of Insecurity on Trade, Markets, and Investment in Rural Nigeria', Report prepared for DFID Nigeria, 2005.
14. Okonta, 'Behind the Mask', 13.

Notes to Response to Chapter 5

1. 'Are Gains on Land Real?', *The Standard*, 19 November 2005.
2. Maurice Odhiambo Makoloo, *Kenya: Minorities, Indigenous Peoples and Ethnic Diversity* (London: Minority Rights Group International, 2005), 2.
3. ILO 169 Indigenous and Tribal Peoples Convention (1989).
4. See L. Hughes, *Moving the Maasai: A Colonial Misadventure* (London: Palgrave Macmillan, 2006) for the source of all quotations.

Notes to Chapter 6

1. W. Beinart and R. Kingwill, 'Eastern Cape Land Reform Pilot Project Pre-planning Report', Working paper 25, Land and Agriculture Policy Centre, Johannesburg, October 1995. Other members of the research team included Maura Andrew, Lungisile Ntsebeza, Silumko Sogoni, and Luvuyo Wotshela. We drew on work by Border Rural Committee staff, especially Mike Kenyon, Siyabulela Manona, Sandra McIntyre, Fanelwa Mhaga, Godfrey Ngqendesha, and Janet Small. Wiebe Nauta, *The Implications of Freedom: the Changing Role of Land Sector NGOs in a transforming South Africa* (Berlin: Lit Verlag, 2004).
2. Department of Land Affairs, 'Introduction Manual for Provincial Steering Committees: Eastern Cape', 27 March 1995.
3. Gallawater, a farm in the pilot area bought by a community in 1995, under Act 126 of 1993, cost R717 per ha.
4. Department of Land Affairs, 'Introduction Manual', 21.
5. Cosmas Desmond, *The Discarded People: an Account of African Resettlement in South Africa* (Harmondsworth: Penguin, 1971); Lauren Platzky and Cherryl Walker, *The Surplus People: Forced Removals in South Africa* (Johannesburg: Ravan Press, 985); Luvuyo Wotshela, 'Homeland Consolidation, Resettlement and Local Politics in the Border and Ciskei Region of the Eastern Cape, South Africa, 1960 to 1996', unpublished D.Phil. thesis, University of Oxford (2001).
6. Lungisile Ntsebeza, 'Social Survey of Thornhill', unpublished draft report to the Border Rural Committee, January 1995. Researchers surveyed every fifth house and, with an average of 5.59 people per household, reached the conclusion that there may have been only 8,000 people resident there at the time. But they considered this an underestimate; and many 'absentees' were at work outside Thornhill.
7. Francis Wilson and Mamphela Ramphele, *Uprooting Poverty: the South African Challenge* (New York: W.W. Norton, 1989),

p. 45; F. Kruger, 'The Legacy of "Homeland" Policy' in M. Ramphele (ed.), *Restoring the Land: Environment and Change in Post-Apartheid South Africa* (London: Panos, 1991); Wotshela, 'Homeland Consolidation'.

8. A further 9,000 ha. was reserved for a game farm, in which neighbouring settlements had some stake, and game reserve; figures from Ciskei government documents.
9. It was difficult to find average holdings because some owners had property elsewhere. A block of nine farms in the priority area for the pilot scheme was offered for sale in 1994: it covered about 7,400 ha. or an average of 822 ha. Most included irrigable fields. Farms in the ring around RA 60 and Zweledinga varied from about 504 ha. to 2,439 ha.
10. The following paragraphs are drawn from BRC documents, discussions, attendance at meetings, and interviews.
11. Siyabu Manona, 'Unravelling Conflicting Land Claims around Hewu', BRC document, 1995.
12. Operation Hunger, 'Report on the Meeting held between Operation Hunger, the Executive Committee of the Civic (SANCO) of Tambo village, and Mr M de Beer, STK'. For broader discussion of Operation Hunger's survey work and 'Participatory Poverty Assessment' see Edward N. Breslin and Peter Delius, 'A Comparative Analysis of Poverty and Malnutrition in South Africa', Operation Hunger, Johannesburg, February 1996.
13. Care must be taken in equating allocated sites with resident households; structures were not complete on all the sites by mid-1995.
14. Wilson and Ramphele, *Uprooting Poverty*, 45.
15. Material from reports by Luvuyo Wotshela, especially 'Preliminary Report on Zweledinga and Some Neighbouring Hewu Comminities', BRC document.
16. Operation Hunger, 'Report on Meeting', April 1995.

17. Rural Support Services, 'Survey of Thornhill: Existing Water Infrastructure', Interim Report, June 1995.
18. Ntsebeza, 'Social Survey'.
19. For a vivid account of agrarian conflct in South Africa, see Jonny Steinberg, *Midlands* (Johannesburg: Jonathan Ball Publishers, 2002).
20. During 1994/5, Queenstown pound was being surrounded by informal settlements on the commonage and by no means secure. Its fences had been cut and repaired so many times that it was beginning to appear naturalized in its shack surroundings. (The new Transitional Local Council promised financial backing for upgrading.) W. Beinart, 'Notes on Queenstown Commonage', BRC document, April 1995.
21. Ntsebeza, 'Social Survey of Thornhill'; Operation Hunger, 'Data Analysis'.
22. J. P. H. Acocks, *Veld Types of South Africa* (Pretoria, 1975) second edition, 51–2; R. D. Barnes, D. L. Flitter and S. J. Milton, *Acacia karroo*, Tropical Forestry Papers, 32 (Oxford, 1996).
23. Ben Cousins, 'Livestock Production and Common Property Struggles in South Africa's Agrarian Reform', *Journal of Peasant Studies*, 23: 2 & 3 (1996), 166–208.
24. C. M. Shackleton, 'Are the Communal Grazing Lands in Need of Saving?', *Development Southern Africa*, 10: 1 (1993), 65–78.
25. For example, Katherine Homewood and W. A. Rodgers, 'Pastoralism, Conservation and the Overgrazing Controversy' in D. Anderson and R. Grove (eds), *Conservation in Africa: People, Policies and Practice* (Cambridge University Press: Cambridge, 1987), 111–28.
26. For these debates see Ben Cousins (ed.), *At the Crossroads: Land and Agrarian Reform in South Africa into the 21st Century* (University of Western Cape: Programme for Land and Agrarian Studies, 2000).
27. Michael Lipton, Mike de Klerk and Merle Lipton, *Land Labour and Livelihoods in Rural South Africa*, 2 volumes (Durban:

Indicator Press, 1996); William Beinart and Colin Murray, 'Agrarian Change, Population Movements and Land Reform in the Free State', Population and Environment Research Programme of the ODA, August 1995, Land and Agriculture Policy Centre, Working Paper 51 (LAPC, Johannesburg, 1996).

28. Beinart and Murray, 'Agrarian Change'.
29. E. Nel, T. Hill, and T. Binns, 'Development from Below in the "New" South Africa: the Case of Hertzog, Eastern Cape', *The Geographical Journal*, 163: 1 (1997); and 'Learning from the People: Participatory Rural Appraisal, Geography and Rural Development in the "New" South Africa', *Applied Geography*, 17: 1 (1997).
30. Chris de Wet, 'Report on a Diagnostic Evaluation Study of the Slovo Welcome Trust Farms in the Whittlesea/Queenstown Area of the Eastern Cape Province', unpublished report, LAPC, January 1998.
31. L. Wotshela, 'Diagnostic Evaluation of Gallawater', unpublished report for Department of Land Affairs, October 1997.
32. Cherryl Walker, 'The Limits to Land Reform: Rethinking the Land Question', *Journal of Southern African Studies*, 31: 4 (2005), 805–24; Deborah James, *Gaining Ground? "Rights" and "Property" in South African Land Reform* (Johannesburg: Wits University Press, 2006).

Index